Daddy Hold

Daddy Hold

Life is a gift. Hold it dearly.

David R. Landis

To the three ladies in my life...

Mom,

you encouraged me to write this story.

Deb,

I will never forget your loving and sacrificial care
for Darla.

Diana,

you were like a second mom to Darla and the best
sister and roommate she could have ever had.

Table of Contents

Prologue

How long, Lord? Will you forget me forever?
How long will you hide your face from me?
How long must I wrestle with my thoughts
and day after day have sorrow in my heart?

Psalm 13:1-2

Night was falling when I drove into the long and winding stony lane that led to my friend's rustic cabin in the beautiful mountains of Blue Ridge, Georgia. It has been my custom to find a secluded spot one weekend each year to spend some time in solitude and reflection, and this was the weekend for that. Before continuing up the hill to the cabin, I stopped in front of his house and got out of my car. Del and his dogs were out on the porch and immediately came down the stairs and walked towards me.

We greeted. Del then informed me that plans had changed and his cabin was no longer available. However, he had made arrangements with the neighbor across the street to allow me to use their vacant vacation home. I was a bit taken aback at the sudden change of plans, but soon followed him in his pickup back out of their lane and onto the mountain highway. Almost directly across the street we made a left turn into another winding but shorter driveway and proceeded back to a secluded but very cozy looking cottage.

I was not disappointed when we walked through the front door. Open ceiling, fireplace, pine flooring, thoughtfully placed accents – all gave the feel of a rustic but well-kept lodge. Del showed me the basic things I would need to know to have a comfortable stay, then wished me a good night and left to return to his house.

I would be all alone for the next several days. Not that I minded that. Only this time would be different. In addition to my normal reading, prayer, reflection, journaling, and walks out in nature, I would also be working through some of the grieving that needed to happen in relation to the death of our daughter less than two months before.

And that is exactly what happened the next day. As I began to reflect on the events of the last several months, a dam broke loose within me. I did not even try to stop it. I knew it was good for me, but I did not expect it to hurt so badly. I paced from room to room, at times clenching my fists and crying out to God with all of the "Why?" questions. "Why did it have to happen this way?" "Why with so much pain?" "Why my precious daughter?" The answers did not come in a blinding flash of light. But as the hours turned into days, the weight of the searing pain lifted its terrible load just a bit. A gentle peace began to invade the bleeding recesses of my heart, and I came to a decision point about something that my mom had been asking of me for quite some time.

Mom has always been like a personal cheerleader through the ups and downs of my life. Always encouraging. Always proud of my accomplishments. And for a good number of years now she's been telling me that I needed to write a book. I always gave her the same answer. "I don't think I have enough life experience, and I don't think I really have enough of a story to tell yet." I could no longer say that. Being alone at the cabin on this particular weekend was what it took for the switch to go on. I was going to write a story. One that I would not have asked to be a part of. Yet, having lived it, I'm forever grateful to the One who authored it.

I was now feeling compelled to share what I pray will be a story of redemption—of hope and faith born out of pain and loss. Darla's story. Our story. God's story. A story to remind each of us that every life is precious, every day is numbered, and quite simply, that some things do not go the way we thought they would, or should, have gone. If, by God's grace, you are in any way encouraged in your journey, or even more importantly, you come to know in a new or deeper way the transforming power of our Lord and Savior Jesus

Christ, then this labor of love will have accomplished its task.

In the storyline of each of our lives there are days that stand out as uniquely different, or special, or painful, and most definitely memorable. This was one of those days.

1. Winds of Change

What is God's will for my life? I ask that you pray with me that I may continue to seek the will of God, and then having found it, to be completely submissive to it, regardless of the cost involved.

Ray D. Landis (my dad), in a letter written to his family on Dec. 14, 1960, having completed one year of Mennonite Voluntary Service in Puerto Rico. He would remain for eight more years.

Friday, August 24, 2012. On that day, 24 was forever etched into our family history. This number would eventually be carved into a tombstone. No longer thought of as two dozen, no longer remembered as Jeff Gordon's race car number, it would just be 24.

Daddy Hold

It was on this day, after a very restless night, that my wife Debbie and I woke up with incredibly heavy hearts, knowing it would be our twelve-year-old-daughter's last day on this earth. You see, on the Wednesday before, in the most emotionally tumultuous space of several hours that I have ever known, we'd come to a decision to remove Darla from the machines that were keeping her unresponsive body alive. Obviously, no parent would ever want to be in this position. Yet we knew that an underlying peace had come into our hearts about this decision, and that in itself was a gift from God. Today, we were going to usher Darla Joy into the arms of Jesus.

Just over one month earlier, we'd left our three oldest children at our home in Atmore, Alabama, and traveled the three and one-half hours north to Birmingham for a "routine" brain surgery that was hoped to give Darla some relief from a lifelong seizure disorder. We were expecting to be back home within a week, but had not been home since. Today would be our 32nd and last day at Children's of Alabama.

These 32 days had encompassed the most sorrow-filled experience I have ever known. To be honest, I did not even know what sorrow was before this. I mean the deep kind of sorrow. A pain that runs so deep it is hard to describe—an unrelenting feeling of intense sadness that stays with you, like an unwelcome guest. Yet it was part of a journey that offered no detours or shortcuts. It just was what it was.

Darla was our fourth child, born three months after moving my pregnant wife Debbie and our children, Diana, David, and Darren, from Green Lane, Pennsylvania to Atmore, Alabama. I was to begin serving as a full-time prison chaplain with a prison ministry headquartered deep in the heart of Dixie. Even now, I marvel at the way God orchestrated events and experiences to completely redirect the trajectory of our family's path to bring us to this point.

Looking back, one couldn't argue with the fact that life was going well for us, at least by all outward appearances. I had a stable Christian walk, happy wife and children, Godly parents, quality friends, solid church family, and a self-started business that was growing in reputation and profit. We really were living the evangelical version of the "American Dream." While this was mostly good, the activities and work schedule I had become accustomed to were arranged in such a way that very little quiet and unplanned time was available. But in those rare moments of reflection, I noticed a stirring was beginning to take place, and in my thought life the frequency of sensing that something different was in store for me was slowly increasing.

Years went by, the pace of life increased, and despite continuing business "success," I found myself asking Debbie questions like "Do you see us doing this for the rest of our lives?" Inside, I was thinking, "There has to be more!" I began to notice that church, marital, and family relationships were being affected by the way I was organizing my priorities. Everything revolved around the business, and what was left for others was truly "left-over."

A significant turning point occurred in 1997. Promise Keepers, a Christian men's movement, was holding a massive one-day rally at the Washington Monument, and a group of us decided to go. The combination of powerful messages, the imagery of such a vast multitude of men calling out to God for wisdom and guidance, and the experience of corporate worship and repentance for our sins and those of our forefathers made a lasting impression on me. I knew that my life needed renewed direction and focus. During our ride home, several in our van load agreed that beginning each work week with Bible study and prayer together would be a good first step in becoming the kind of husbands, fathers, and workers that God wanted us to be.

Beginning at 5:30 a.m. on the following Monday and each week thereafter, friends, co-workers, and business associates gathered around a workbench in my sign shop and shared testimonies, scripture, and prayer. It was a season of listening, learning, and reflecting. One particular Monday morning, after we'd been meeting together for over a year, my life's direction took a dramatic turn. The men who were a part of the prayer group had left for their respective workplaces. Only my brother Alvin remained.

Alvin and I had been working together since the early years of the business, and having both experienced the recent birth of a child (their first and our third), we began to reflect on our roles as Christian fathers and husbands. We soon came to the conclusion that in order to remain faithful to God's plan and design for our families, our priorities would have to be drastically adjusted. Although several options were discussed, the only one that "felt right" was a radical decision to significantly downsize our operation by discontinuing a major line of our work. We were both fully aware that it could potentially impact Alvin's employment status. A time of prayer sealed the decision in our hearts.

Looking back, I know that Monday morning act of consecration and surrender was one of those special, holy moments in life. I was about to find out that the effects of that decision would have far reaching implications, not only for me, but for everyone connected to our family. Although current work order commitments would all be honored, I drafted and mailed a letter explaining our decision to hundreds of current customers. In our success-driven community, what we were doing looked like a big step backwards. So as news of our decision spread, family, friends, business associates and fellow church members began to ask questions. Generally, there was support for the idea, but many questioned and some even ridiculed our decision. Although I wrestled with some of the negative responses, I felt very strongly that this was the direction God wanted me to go.

Almost immediately, I sensed a greater need for God's presence, a deeper hunger for His Word, and a growing realization that my life's journey was about to take some interesting turns, though I had no idea what they might be. Several months later, my brother and I were working on a truck lettering job away from the shop. As we worked, the idea came to me that it would be good to spend some time studying the Bible in a more formal setting. It felt like the only way this would work would be to step away from the business for a period of time, immerse myself in Biblical studies and listen to what God might be saying to us as a family. I walked over to where my brother was working and hesitantly asked him what he thought of the idea. "Would you be willing to manage the business for a brief season if we should decide to pursue this route?" I asked. He readily agreed.

That same week, after receiving counsel from several friends, I, along with Debbie and the children, took an exploratory trip to Rosedale Bible College in Ohio. We wanted to get a sense if this was something we should pursue. We arrived on campus, and not finding the host couple from whom we were supposed to get the key for our room, we walked out into the yard where a family was playing in the grass. We introduced ourselves, explained our reason for being there, and before long were invited into their living quarters.

For the next few hours we exchanged testimonies in wonder of how God was uniquely drawing and calling our families to follow after Him more wholeheartedly, no matter the cost, and wherever He might lead us. Again, there was the sense that God was orchestrating events and adding substance to our faith as we began journeying into new territories. As we concluded our visit and walked to our room, Debbie and I looked at each other. Both of us knew that something was up.

Enrollment was the next step, and several months later our family was temporarily situated in an apartment on the school's campus while I took in various Biblical studies. During that first semester, I "happened" to be in a class taught by Phil Weber, the president of a prison ministry in Alabama called We Care Program. I had never met Phil, nor did I know anything of We Care Program. Because of the small size of the class that semester, it didn't take long for a friendship to develop between Phil and myself.

One morning, over breakfast at a local restaurant, we entered into a discussion about how to discern God's call, ministry in general, and other life issues I was trying to work through in my own mind. Then it came. Yes. "The Invitation." Would I consider being part of a week-long prison crusade in Alabama!? One thing I can say for sure. Prison ministry was not on my radar. I had never even heard of We Care Program before this Bible study experiment, and Alabama!? Yeah, right! But the invitation had been delivered...and all I could say was "I'll have to think about that." (I might have said I'll pray about it, but there wasn't much to pray about...I knew I was going!)

2.   The Call

Do you not say, 'There are still four months
and then comes the harvest'?
Behold, I say to you, lift up your eyes and look at the
fields, for they are already white for harvest!

John 4:35 (NKJV)

S everal months later I was on a bus headed to
Alabama along with my brother and two
friends. We were ready to participate in our
first prison crusade. I wondered, "What in the world am
I doing on a bus full of radicals traveling 1000 miles to
talk to some guys in a prison in Alabama?" What a trip
it was – beginning with the experience of our bus
fishtailing across the frozen interstate to avoid a jack-

13

knifed tractor trailer (we came to a stop just in front of
the truck as cars veered around the bus to avoid hitting
us), then being stranded at a truck stop through the
night. What was usually a twenty-hour ride turned into
thirty. God seemed to be saying to me, "Get ready! This
will not be a normal week, but I will be with you."

It truly was a life-changing week! The theme of the
event, "Proclaiming Jesus, Friend of Sinners," opened
my eyes to see prisoners not for what they had done, but
for what God had done for them (and us!). I felt so
unprepared to share this message of Hope. I was not
one to quickly go out of my way to "share the Gospel"
as I understood evangelism to be in those days. But as
our ministry team gathered for teaching, encouragement, and prayer each morning, God gave me the
needed words and empowerment for each day.

Walking into the prison on the first day was a totally
new experience for me. I sensed darkness surrounding
me, but even in the midst of it, I was at peace knowing
that God was present and in control. Each day God led
me to different men who needed someone to talk with,
listen, or pray for them. I also sensed a burden for the
"Church" in the prison, seeing how they needed
someone to help with encouraging and discipling those
who were new in their walk with the Lord. It was both
the hardest and the most fulfilling week of my life.

As the week went on, God began to tug at my heart.
My eyes were opened to the need for laborers in the
harvest fields of Alabama's prison system. I was made
aware that the doors were wide open to additional

The Call

volunteer chaplains. Then, in one of our morning gatherings as a team, a man named Cecil Montgomery sang a song that would change the course of my life.

The song, "My House is Full,"[1] painted a picture of a church filled with peace, food, singing, and laughter. Outside were fields of grain ready for harvest. In the distance, the Father sadly cries "My house is full, but my field is empty, who will go and work for Me today?" Inside, no one was willing to push away from the table to work in the fields. No one was willing to reap the harvest.

The song ended with this question: "Who will go and work in my fields?" I felt conviction. I was one who was sitting at the table. As the song came to a close I surrendered my will to God's will, whatever that might be. (Some would say that this is when I received the "call" to ministry.) It was time for me to push myself away from the table—get up—and go.

It was certainly not a coincidence that the very prison I was serving in for the week, J.O. Davis Correctional Center, and the 400 men who lived there, had need of an assistant chaplain to work alongside its chaplain, J.R. Yoder. (J.R. "happened" to be the father of the family we'd met and shared testimonies with during our exploratory visit to the Bible College in Ohio!)

Needless to say, the experiences of that week began what would become a radical reorientation of our family's future. One by one, extended family, home, church, community, and ultimately, the business I had started eleven years earlier were all left behind to answer God's call to visit those in prison. Initially, we

---

[1] Lanny Wolfe, 1977

committed to a one-year term of service. That was in 1999, and like they say, the rest is history.

Little did we realize that the greatest challenges to come would have nothing to do with entering full-time prison ministry, something about which I knew very little, felt quite unprepared for, and was somewhat overwhelmed by. We were soon to learn that our greatest suffering would center around the birth and impending special needs of our fourth child, Darla Joy.

3. "Special Needs"

One thing I am learning. Every person has a handicap.
Some are just more severe.

Journal, 2006

Darla's entry into the world was not without
concern. It had not been a "normal"
pregnancy. A difficult labor turned into an
emergency C-section. Early complications with Darla's
kidneys and urinary tract system precipitated a transfer
from the local hospital where she was born to a larger
hospital one hour away.

At six months of age, Darla had her first visible
seizure. This, of course, was very frightening to us, but
unfortunately, it was only the beginning of what would

became a long and grueling twelve-year journey of sickness, hospitalizations, medicine, procedures, tests, therapy, and little in the form of solid answers.

Two years after Darla was born, I penned the following in my journal:

> *The last several days have been somewhat of a valley as Debbie and I slowly come to the realization that Darla's condition is more serious than we thought. We understand the kidney problems, and we can handle the seizures, but is there also a mental disorder?*
>
> *Because of [Darla's] lack of development in speech, coordination, etc., it seems that something much different is going on here...We must somehow rest in the fact that God knows best and has chosen us to care for this special child of His.*
>
> *Oh, how we need His strength to carry on, though. Questions about the future and what she will be like dominate our thinking, and again we must come back to living one hour at a time. For if we knew what the future held, how could we accept it?*
>
> *For now, thank You for our precious Darla. Help us to see You in her. Help us to hear You through her. Help us to know You better because of her. Help us to care more. But most of all, help us.*

As a father, I felt totally helpless and was often discouraged, longing to "fix" whatever was wrong with my little girl. Over the years, we'd exhausted every possible avenue in our search for answers: just about every kind of seizure medication, two trips to Miami Children's Hospital for extensive evaluations, the

Ketogenic Diet, and a Vagus Nerve Stimulator implant. Nothing seemed to bring sustained relief.

As Darla grew, her condition gradually deteriorated. There was never a diagnosis, so we affectionately called her condition "Darla Syndrome." For most of Darla's life she was not able to talk, walk, feed, or take care of her own basic needs.

I will never forget the day that I saw Darla sitting in her first wheelchair. I had just come home from work,

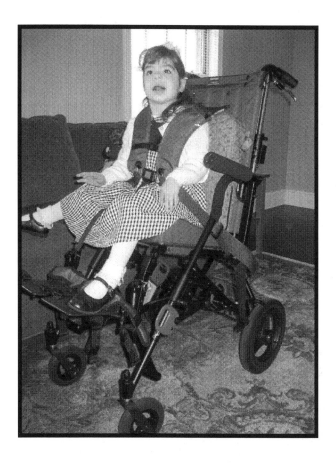

and Debbie was quick to point my attention to the brand new, specially designed piece of medical equipment. We'd been waiting for months for the wheelchair to arrive. Up until this point some may have wondered why our growing daughter was still spending so much time in an all-terrain child's stroller. She had definitely outgrown it.

Now, as she proudly sat in her new carrier, there was no question about her condition – she was different, and would likely always be different. Titles like "Handicapped," "Special Needs," "Retarded," and "Mentally Challenged" came to the forefront of my mind as I tried to take in what would in time become "normal" for our family.

I was almost shocked by how big the purple wheelchair was, and the fact that my youngest daughter was sitting in it didn't really help any. As if that weren't enough, it was obviously designed with adjustment points ready to expand or lengthen as her body grew over time.

One particular detail bothered me the most. It was the way her shoes were strapped down with wide black nylon straps making it impossible for her to kick her legs up and down like she wanted to. I was always self-conscious in public settings about the amount "kicking" noise she made. Now I just wanted her to kick to her heart's content – make all the noise she wanted to make!

I don't know if I cried that day, but I know I felt like crying. It was one of many "reality check" moments in the years of caring for Darla. Obviously, there was still a lot of room for growth in my heart.

"Special Needs"

It has taken me years to understand with greater maturity the way that God sees each and every one of us. I am learning that every human being is created in the image of God, has a purpose and a plan designed and ordained by God, and that, no matter his or her limitations, is valuable in God's sight.

4. Grasping for Answers

It is a moment-by-moment spiritual experience to deny the urge to self-pity. Most of the time I walk in victory, but other times I give in to an attitude or moment of depression. I want to be able to ask God "Why not more trouble in our lives?" instead of "Why so much trouble?" We, in our sinful moments, are certainly deserving of the worst that could come, but because of the mercy of God, the worst has not befallen us. We still live, and God gives us enough strength for the battles of each day. "My grace is sufficient for you."

Journal, 2005

Even though Darla was born with a number of health issues that presented us with a variety of challenges early on, I initially (and I guess with some ignorance) held on to the belief that the problems Darla was having would at some point work themselves out; that she would somehow grow out of whatever was holding her back. In her younger years Darla actually looked very healthy and was growing nicely. I remained optimistic that with medicine, and perhaps with some kind of supernatural intervention, my fourth child would eventually catch up to the other three in her level of development.

I was serving as a full time prison chaplain during the early years of Darla's life. A popular teaching in prison settings, both through media and print and with some of the volunteers who came in was the "health and wealth gospel." This was a message I never felt completely right about. To the men in prison, it sounded good, taught well, and produced a lot of emotion. The promise of a better "whatever" was something they could cling to, even though the reality of it was rarely, if ever, seen or experienced. Of course, the prison teacher or volunteer went home, the weekly TV or radio episode came to a close, and the inmate had no other option but to go back to the filth and discouragement of prison life. Eventually, faith in this concept would run dry and in time it was back to what worked before – survival of the fittest, every man for himself. So much for this "God-thing," they would say, "It doesn't work"

This feel good teaching actually carried me for a short while. I was going to "name it and claim it" for Darla! God was going to come through for us, and everything was going to be OK. But Darla's condition did not improve. In fact, we began to see a gradual deterioration over time. In one extremely discouraging two-year stretch, Darla was admitted to the hospital over 25 times, not including quite a number of emergency room visits. Doctors, therapists, tests, treatments, and medicine became a normal part of our lives.

If it would have been possible for me to wear a monitor that would have let others know what was going on inside of me, I am not sure what they would have thought. On any given day I might be hanging on to the verse that says "my God shall supply all my needs according to His riches in glory" (Phil. 4:19), and in the next moment I might be looking for a place to get away to so I could cry out some tears. Was I growing hardened and faithless in my understanding of the ways of God?

Certainly, in our journey with Darla, the "feel good" meter did not always go up and to the right. What we were experiencing with Darla was not our idea of what "normal" should have looked like. Then again, maybe our idea of normal just needed to change.

With a deeper resolve to understand the ways of God, I slowly began to work through the issues of suffering and pain – the "why?" questions. It was an ongoing struggle and argument with God, not in the sense of doubting my salvation or His unfathomable power, but as an intimate battle raging deep inside. I searched the scriptures, listened to messages, read books, prayed, asked for prayer at times, and all the while watched as Darla's health and quality of life continued to decline.

I remember well the evening my family and I went in for the evening service at J. O. Davis Correctional

Center. Darla was less than a year old at the time, and everything about the way things were going was not looking good for her. Darla was struggling with kidney problems that caused constant urinary tract infections. This was later corrected with surgery, but at this point our lives were centered on keeping Darla as comfortable as possible from one period of sickness to the next.

We'd just returned from a family trip to Pennsylvania. On the twenty-hour drive back to Alabama, we noticed Darla was not feeling well. We soon discovered that she had fever, which basically meant another urinary tract infection was brewing. Needless to say, we were tense and nervous. We still had a long way to go. Fortunately, with a steady diet of Motrin, we were able to finish the trip and scheduled an appointment with Darla's urologist the following day, Friday. The doctor changed her antibiotic, and we were told to come back on Monday.

Our family was scheduled to go into the prison for the evening chapel service on Saturday, the day after the doctor visit. We were somewhat discouraged as it seemed that every time our scheduled service came around on the calendar either Darla or someone else got sick and we were not able to go in as a family. We debated what we should do, then decided to go in. But instead of conducting our usual service, we decided to conduct a healing service!

It was one of those nights that you never forget. I remember being up front sharing the message and looking into the front row. There was my family, surrounded by my closest inmate friends, one of them holding little Darla like a proud grandfather. People have asked if I ever feared taking my family in for prison services. I guarantee you in those moments Darla was as safe as ever. These men were protecting her like she was royalty! I finished the message and then proceeded, with the help of several inmate church leaders, to lead in a healing service.

Now I will have to admit that at this stage of our journey I was still pretty confident that God was going to heal Darla and restore her to full health, so I was not afraid to boldly ask God for healing in a service like this. However, I wanted the inmate elders to be the ones to anoint Darla with oil and pray for her healing, probably because I felt they possessed more faith than I. Together, we lifted Darla before the throne of grace and asked God to heal her from infection and restore her to full health. It was a very moving time and opened the way for many in that service to come forward for prayer and anointing for various needs and concerns. We were not surprised on the following Monday when Darla's urology doctor informed us that Darla's infection had cleared up, at least for the time being.

Several days later my inmate friend Billy Don walked into my office and handed me the following poem he had written after the service:

Darla Joy,

As I looked deep within your eyes,
You looked right back at me to my surprise.

So large and pure, with lots of love,
I could tell right away; you were sent from
God above.

Daddy Hold

I was so scared when your mom handed you my way,
    But, when I held you, why it was like I had
    been doing it every day.

You were so warm and soft and you smelled so good,
    All those soap companies would love to have
    that smell if they could.

You fell asleep and you slept for a while,
    I just sat right there with a great big smile,

Your dad preached a sermon on Psalm 23,
    But all through his sermon, you were all that
    I could see.

I looked at your hands so perfect and small,
    The most beautiful little hands as I could ever recall,

And it became very clear why God made us all.

The evening passed so quickly and came to an end,
    And I hope very much that I've made a
    life-long friend.

Please always remember as you grow, Darla Joy,
    That on February 19th, the year 2000,
    you brought this old man lots and lots of joy.

Your faithful admirer, Billy Don

5. Suffering Together

Many of us are tempted to think that if we suffer, the only important thing is to be relieved of our pain. We want to flee it at all costs. But when we learn to move through suffering, rather than avoid it, then we greet it differently. We become willing to let it teach us. We even begin to see how God can use it for some larger end. Suffering becomes something other than a nuisance or curse to be evaded at all costs, but a way into deeper fulfillment. Ultimately, mourning means facing what wounds us in the presence of One who can heal."[2]

Henri Nouwen

---

[2] Henri Nouwen, *Turn My Mourning into Dancing: Finding Hope in Hard Times* (Nashville: W Publishing Group, A Division of Thomas Nelson, Inc., 2011), xv.

Daddy Hold

Other inmate and former inmate friends also prayed for and expressed concern for Darla. On one occasion I had lunch with two friends, both of whom were former inmates. One of them I had last seen ten years earlier when he was a student in one of my prison classes.

Our time together was very encouraging. I was especially grateful to hear that my friend whom I had not seen for so long was doing well and walking with Jesus. But one thing stood out to me in that conversation. At one point, he asked me about Darla's well-being. I was surprised to know he clearly remembered the times over ten years ago when I shared with my students how things were going in my family and particularly the challenges we were facing in the early stages of our daughter's journey with epilepsy.

It was common for the men in the class to share words of comfort and commit to pray for Darla. But what touched me on this day was when my friend thanked me, with tears in his eyes, for giving him the opportunity to pray for my family, and Darla in particular, while he was in prison. Yes, he was deeply grateful for the Bible studies and classes. He thanked me for those too. However, something about getting on an equal level with our shared life experiences seemed to bring about a sense of oneness in Christ, and I think that's what he remembered and appreciated the most.

Twelve years later, with many healing services and prayers in between, another special anointing took place in our kitchen. (This was just a few months before making the decision to take Darla to Children's of Alabama in Birmingham.) Frank, a former inmate and friend of mine, was burdened for Darla. He was a faithful participant in a weekly men's prayer group from the local First Assembly of God Church. One day he came to me and asked if Debbie and I would be ok with him bringing this prayer group to our house to anoint Darla with oil and have a prayer of healing for her.

By that point in our journey we'd accepted the situation for what it was. Although we so badly wanted to see freedom from seizures for Darla, we'd long since stopped praying for "healing" and hoped instead for small signs of improvement or special graces for the daily challenges that all of us faced, especially Darla. It was also during this time that we were considering the options that eventually led us to Birmingham. So it was no problem for us to open our home to this group of prayer warriors if they wanted to pray for Darla's healing. We'd never turned down prayer! A date was scheduled for the group to come over.

The experience was just another of many special and memorable moments in our journey with Darla. About seven or eight men, including Frank, showed up around 7:00 p.m. on that Monday night. After initial greetings and handshakes, they were ready to pray. We pushed Darla over in her wheelchair and parked her in the middle of the group. The men laid hands on her and began to pray in a unified concert of praise and prayer to God.

I remember standing back and discreetly taking a picture of what was transpiring. Darla was totally surrounded by this group of dear brothers in Christ, so much so, that she is not even visible in the picture. Just a group of men hovering over a special little girl, all at the impulse of my friend Frank, who only several years prior was crying out to God to save him from the mess he had made out of his life.

We experienced many other similar encounters over the years, both in and out of prison. There was no doubt that thoughts were turned in a spiritual direction when people were around Darla, both children and adults alike. In fact, our experiences with Darla in many ways shaped and defined who I was becoming and how I approached life and ministry. Nevertheless, our journey with Darla created a constant source of tension within me when it came to matters associated with healing and prayer.

6.   Prayer Requests

Father, if you are willing, take this cup from me;
yet not my will, but yours be done.

Luke 22:42

As time progressed and Darla's condition worsened I became more and more uncomfortable with knowing how or what to ask others to pray for in relation to Darla's health condition. Being immersed in a "full-time" ministry culture since just before Darla's birth had opened my eyes to the variety of ways in which Christians (and non-Christians) view prayer.

Daddy Hold

Over the years my family and I have seen and experienced everything from prayer cloths to prayer vigils, loud and almost demanding prayers to tearful and "unsure how to pray" prayers, prisoner prayers to preacher prayers, and everything in between. We have no doubt that all have been well meaning, and have seen and experienced the hand of God bringing grace to our circumstances time and time again in small and meaningful ways. At the same time, we became very aware that Darla's special needs and health difficulties had been a significant part of our "sanctification" as we wrestled with God over questions of faith and trust.

During one season of intense struggle I decided to dig around in Scripture to see what I could learn (again) about prayer, particularly what should be the emphasis and longing of our prayer requests. I am not a theologian, nor do I have all of the answers on this issue, but this is what I discovered: I pray a lot more about God doing something FOR me than Him doing something IN me!

I did not find this to be the case in many of the examples of prayer in the New Testament. There, petitioners prayed that their fellow believers would know God and His power better (Eph. 1:15-21). They longed for the Church to be rooted and established in love, filled to the measure of all the fullness of God (Eph. 3:14-19). That brothers and sisters would abound more and more in love, and that they would be pure and blameless until the day of Christ, filled with the fruit of righteousness (Phil. 1:3-6, 9-11). They prayed for God's power to help them live a life worthy of the Lord, one that would please Him in every way, bearing fruit in every good work (Col. 1:9-14).

36

Then, when early believers asked others to pray for them, they asked for boldness in proclaiming the Gospel (Eph. 6:19-20), open doors so that the message of God would spread rapidly (Col. 4:2-4, 2 Thess. 3:1) and that God would work in them what was pleasing to Him (Hebrews 13:18-21).

In general, I found that Biblical intercessions were focused on personal righteousness, Spirit-infused power, and unhindered boldness in proclaiming Christ. Ultimately, prayer was about God and His will being foremost, hearts being transformed into the likeness of His Son, and God being glorified in all things!

Not so with how I saw myself and those around me calling out to God. I am embarrassed to think of the times that my agenda was (and still is at times) at the forefront of my prayers. That I would have a "good" day. That things would go "well." That hardship would be removed. That my pathway would be unhindered. That my plans would succeed. That God would pour His blessings into my life. That sickness and pain would disappear. Not that any or all of these things would not be okay, but were they really what was most important in God's Kingdom economy?

So how did these revelations re-shape my thinking about prayer? In Luke 18 Jesus gives us the example of the persistent widow to show us that we should always pray and not give up! I'm not going to stop praying for healing in certain situations or asking others to do the same for me. However, these reminders have changed the focus of my praying to less about my personal wants and "needs" and more about my ongoing sanctification.

Could God have brought healing (in the way that we understand healing) to Darla's life? Surely He could have if that is what He wanted. But it became clearer to us over the years that Darla was a gift—a special treasure—a "thorn in the flesh" lovingly allowed by God with the intention of building character and trust in myself, our family, and I suppose in others as well.

Over time, we accepted the lot that had been given to us. Not that we understood it by any stretch, but we learned to be at peace with our situation—to exercise contentment—to realize that no matter what we might be going through we can easily find ourselves groping for something just beyond our reach if we are not careful. And that to me would equal a life of misery.

I gradually came to the place where I made it my duty to get up each day with a hug and a kiss for Darla and in the best way I knew give her all the affection and love I could muster up. The key was to remember that as we moved into a very uncertain future there would always be, by God's grace, strength for each day.

I am very thankful for the prison healing service and the special anointing that happened in our kitchen. I also praise God for everything that happened in between. Each and every experience was instrumental in helping us to see the glory and majesty of God.

I still do not understand why everything turned out the way it did. But one thing I am sure of. Darla is healed.

7.   Facing Limits

Limits are often God's gifts in disguise.

Peter Scazzero

I remember well the feelings I had as Darla's condition was deteriorating in her final years. Watching the level of care that was required to attend to Darla's needs, I began to lament the fact that we might be coming to a place where we were going to have to ask for help. I did not like acknowledging that we were quickly approaching a place of neediness. As someone who had started and operated a business for over ten years, relocated my family from Pennsylvania to Alabama to follow a special calling, and led a growing non-profit ministry for over a decade, I was always the one leading the way.

In addition, Debbie and I were both pretty confident in our own abilities to take care of situations and challenges that presented themselves to us. I think we both had an inner streak of confidence that led us to believe we could handle just about anything – no matter the extent of the challenge or the degree of sacrifice. However, like a reality that creeps up somewhat unexpectedly, then declares itself with a special dose of intensity, we were both beginning to see that caring for Darla in the longer term was looking like it might be bigger than we could manage. Especially if we wanted to be the kind of persons we needed to be for each other, our three older children, and others who were a special part of our lives.

This caused a great deal of angst in my own spirit. In my more "spiritual" moments I had silently pledged my own life and existence to take care of Darla to the end, even to the point of significantly limiting or radically redirecting my work priorities or even stepping down from my leadership position. If it had to be so, I was going to be the "hero" dad who gave everything he had for the benefit of his special needs daughter.

Perhaps this is the calling of some, and I deeply respect what are very personal decisions. Yet as I continued to process in my own mind what was slowly unfolding before us, I came to the realization that we were going to have to ask for help. It was now I who was singing "It's me, it's me, Oh Lord, standing in the need of prayer."[3]

God speaks to us in many ways about things like this – scripture passages, unique life experiences, devotionals or sermons, or sometimes just a quiet knowing. There are also times when God speaks through a friend, and that is what happened in this case.

It had been quite a while since I had gone out for lunch with my friend Jim. Though we were both involved in prison ministry, he lived an hour away and our paths were not crossing as much as they used to. We set up a lunch appointment close to the prison where he conducted a weekly teaching.

As usual, we talked about a lot of different things. Then at one point in the conversation Jim picked up on the fact that Darla's long-term care was becoming a concern to me. He started to dig into that issue, and we soon discovered that my own pride might be getting in the way of asking for help. He challenged me to think about my responsibility to love not only Darla, but also our three other children and maybe even more importantly my own dear wife.

I had always been impressed by Debbie's strength and determination. With God's help she was able to persevere – and keep a joyful attitude despite great sacrifice and pain. Her witness to God's grace was evident to all. In some ways perhaps, Debbie's abilities and character were hiding the fact that it might be time to figure out a way to bring in some reinforcement. I knew that it would take a very special person and a very

---

[3] African-American spiritual, author unknown.

special set of circumstances for a satisfactory Darla care arrangement to come about.

My allowing our family to play "the hero" scenario for Darla might look good in some ways, but was it really the healthiest and most loving solution to what we were facing? Were we really able to give Darla the best possible care in her deteriorating condition? What did true love look like for each family member, including Darla, when considering all of these variables? I was not eager to look into these issues, but Jim's "butt-kicking" got me started on a journey that led to a most beautiful gift.

8. Caring with Dignity

While Jesus was in Bethany in the home of Simon
the Leper, a woman came to him with an alabaster jar
of very expensive perfume, which she poured on his
head as he was reclining at the table.
When the disciples saw this, they were indignant.
"Why this waste?" they asked.
"This perfume could have been sold at a high price
and the money given to the poor."

Matthew 26:6-9

In the bigger story of Darla's life certain events or
seasons stand out as unforgettable markers of
God's grace. What follows is one of those special
gifts.

Our church had recently welcomed an executive

pastor to our leadership team. He and his family had relocated from Pennsylvania, although they had previously lived in Atmore so we knew them fairly well. What we were not aware of was that his wife had some training and experience in working with special needs children and was looking for part-time employment. To cap it off, her name was Darla Joy! (As any good Southerner would do, we will refer to her as "Mrs. Darla" from here on.)

It did not take us long to see that God might be up to something, and we promptly made some connections. Phone calls were made in regards to financial assistance. This, of course, was not something I wanted to do, but I knew it was the right thing, and time revealed God's faithfulness all over again. As a result of the generosity and loving concern of many, our Darla received some very special care in what, unbeknownst to us at the time, was the last year of her life.

Rarely have I ever witnessed such dignity and respect for God's image. Although I was not home for most of the days that Mrs. Darla was at our house, in my comings and goings I couldn't help but notice something very special taking place.

I saw Mrs. Darla reading to our Darla, even making a special effort to show her the pictures in the books she was reading. This was despite the fact that Darla usually did not appear to respond to these kinds of efforts. Sometimes I heard light singing coming from the room they were in. I noticed that our Darla had tremendous peace in her countenance. I observed that mealtimes were not just something to check off a to-do list, but were being made into special experiences for Darla.

The care that struck me as most special though was how Mrs. Darla would conclude Darla's bath time. After allowing Darla plenty of time to enjoy herself in the bathtub, she would gently dry her off and lay her on the changing table. It was then time for Darla to be rubbed down with body lotion.

I remember especially the "heels" of Darla's hands and the "knobs" on her knees. Both were calloused from years of crawling and scooting around on the floor. I know that these areas received special attention, because over time they began to soften up a bit. I will never forget how Darla felt and smelled when I came home from work at the end of one of these special days.

I am certainly not comparing Darla to Jesus, but as I look back over this time I get a sense that Mrs. Darla

was preparing our Darla for her homegoing. I see in her ministry to Darla the same extravagance shown by the sinful woman who anointed the feet of Jesus with outrageously expensive perfume. Some, as in those days, would deem this kind of care a waste of time, energy, and expense. To me as Darla's dad, it was a priceless gift and a treasured memory.

To add blessing to blessing, I even saw that over time Debbie was beginning to experience a lift in her spirits. Twelve years of 24-7 care had taken its toll to some degree. Looking back, we know that God was using this special arrangement to prepare Debbie for the total freedom (and loss) that was coming. We were so touched by this level of care that later, when the time came to plan a memorial service for Darla, we knew that we wanted Mrs. Darla to participate. Her words were as follows:

Many of you knew Darla Joy as the child in the special chair. But if you looked a little deeper, you soon would learn she was a child with spunk, attitude, and yes, even a little stubbornness.

Even though her communication was limited, I knew when she enjoyed having her hair brushed and braided and when she just wasn't in the mood. Bath time was a favorite and it could be an adventure. She loved to splash in the water, but it was an added thrill if I were to be splashed in the process! I would be the one to let out a yelp, and a big broad smile would encompass her face. Darla loved to be held close and read to. Singing would soothe her and walks outside at times would invigorate her.

Perhaps one of the most beautiful treasures Darla Joy had to offer was her ability to show unconditional love and acceptance. And through her disability teach others that it was o.k. to be different. During many visits to my house, Darla Joy had the opportunity to interact with two other very special children—Addie, age 4, and Will, age 3. They loved to touch her, hold her hand, help put her feet on the foot rest of her wheelchair, read stories and when we would go on walks, they would pick beautiful flower "weeds" just for her. Darla Joy would show her excitement by thumping the tray on her wheelchair, lifting her voice in a squeal or showing her contagious smile.

A lot of questions were asked, "Why can't Darla Joy walk? Why can't she talk?" This laid the platform for a conversation of the beauty of our individual uniqueness and how someday, when we get to heaven, God will give us new bodies so we can do the things we were unable to do here on earth. Without a word spoken, God used Darla

Daddy Hold

Joy's life to sow seeds of gentleness, compassion and acceptance of those with "special needs" into the lives of those children.

Over the past few weeks many prayers have been prayed by Addie and Will, asking Jesus to heal Darla. On the afternoon of August 24, my daughter Morgan gathered little Addie and Will into her arms and told them Darla Joy went to live with Jesus. With a smile on her face and glint in her eye, Addie exclaimed, 'SO, NOW SHE CAN WALK!' And Will not missing a beat, 'NOW SHE CAN TALK!'

9. Hope Erased

Why, my soul, are you downcast?
Why so disturbed within me?
Put your hope in God,
for I will yet praise him,
my Savior and my God.

Psalm 42:5

It had been about six months earlier when Debbie and I began to feel that it would be good to get a second opinion on Darla's rapidly deteriorating condition. We'd been seeing the same neurologist for over ten years, and as much as we appreciated the help he had been to us, we felt it was time for a change.

Daddy Hold

Darla was not doing well at all, and we were not sure which direction to go.

In what we believed was an answer to the prayers of many, a connection was made with Dr. Smith, a neurologist in Birmingham, and an initial visit was soon scheduled. Upon hearing our story, Dr. Smith scheduled us for a two-day video EEG (electro-encephalogram) in Birmingham so that she could make her own assessment of Darla's condition based on past history and current realities.

After an extensive evaluation we agreed that a corpus callosotomy might be a worthwhile option. This procedure, sometimes called "split-brain surgery", is reserved for patients with extreme forms of uncontrollable epilepsy. It involves cutting all or part of a band of nerve fibers (corpus callosum) that connect the two halves (hemispheres) of the brain. This would disable communication between the hemispheres and prevent the spread of seizures from one side of the brain to the other. Our next step was to meet with a brain surgeon who could perform the surgery.

Our initial visit with the surgeon was very encouraging. Armed with the results of Darla's most recent tests, Dr. Andrews assured us confidently, and with much encouragement, that a better quality of life was on the way for Darla. Other than the normal cautions about surgery in general, it looked like we were heading towards a win-win situation. In fact, Dr. Andrews was not aware of even one situation out of the 80-some similar surgeries he had performed where the patient did not see improvement.

Hope Erased

The decision seemed pretty clear—we could watch Darla's condition worsen, or we could subject her to this fairly routine brain surgery that promised at least some relief. Needless to say, we were optimistic that something good was about to happen, and it couldn't come soon enough.

There was a sense of cautiously hopeful anticipation as we packed up for the trip to Birmingham. Thoughts of relief for Darla were mixed with concerns about the magnitude of our decision. We were looking forward to a successful surgery and hopefully returning home within a week.

Because of needing to be at the hospital early on the morning of the surgery, we'd decided to get a hotel room the night before. We arrived in decent time, lounged and played with Darla on the king size bed, bathed her, then

all settled in for a night of sleep.

We arrived at the hospital bright and early the next morning. We'd already been thoroughly informed of everything that would be involved, so the preparations seemed fairly routine. But when they came to take Darla to the operating room, I found it difficult to let her go. Every surgery is a serious thing, but even with everything that Darla had already been through during her short life thus far, this one felt weighty. Of course our hope was that everything would go as anticipated and Darla's condition would be improved. But nagging doubts were also present. Would this be the last time we would see Darla in her present state? Could the surgery possibly complicate matters even more?

We were greatly relieved when Dr. Andrews came out to talk to us about eight hours after the surgery had begun. He informed us that from a surgical standpoint, everything had gone perfectly. There had been no complications. But when we finally got to see Darla after a long day of waiting, we knew that something was not right. We could tell just by looking at her eyes, and by the way that her head was tilted to the left. We soon discovered that the results of this surgery were completely opposite of what anybody had expected.

In conversations before the surgery we were told that most patients came out of this particular surgery "stunned" and would lie still for up to several days' seizure free. It was quite evident that Darla did not fit into that mold. Before long, her seizure activity started up again, and over the course of the next few days increased to a level that we'd not seen before.

Watching Darla struggle again was heartbreaking. We'd brought Darla to Birmingham with the hope of relief from the seizures that had racked her body for most of her life. Now hope was beginning to slip away. There were daily, even hourly, discussions with the medical staff. It soon became apparent that our only choice at this point was to allow the doctors to put Darla in a medically induced coma. This would give her some relief from the non-stop seizures she was now

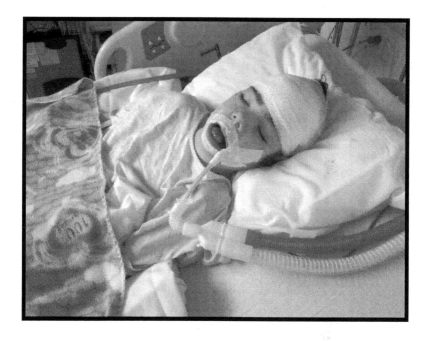

experiencing—and would also give the medical team some time to consider what, and if, any options remained.

We did not know at this point that as the medications took their effect and Darla drifted off into a coma we would never see her eyes open again. And, we did not know that we would soon be left with no other option but to subject Darla to a second and more invasive brain surgery.

In one week Debbie and I had gone from playing with Darla in the hotel room the night before the surgery, to sitting by her comatose body, waiting, wondering, praying, crying and hoping. We were losing hope as parents, and discouragement was setting in. A totally unknown future lay ahead of us. We were at an impasse.

Our journey with Darla was leading us into the valley of the shadow of death.

10. Changing Perspectives

...I was in prison and you came to visit me.

Matthew 25:36b

I can still clearly remember sitting by Darla's bedside in those early days after the first surgery, stunned by the unexpected turn of events. We were 3 ½ hours away from our three older children, our church family, and my ministry colleagues. If that weren't enough, we were also 1000 miles apart from our parents, siblings and their families. We felt lonely and discouraged, and were filled with an ever increasing sorrow.

During one of these moments of despair, a gentle-spirited, soft-spoken man came walking our way for what would be his first of many visits. I remember those initial visits with Chaplain Mark with intrigue. Initially, he kept himself appropriately and professionally distanced. But as the days turned into weeks a friendship began to develop, and I would, with great anticipation, look forward to his daily visits. I wanted to get to know him better. I suppose since we served in similar ministry environments I felt a connection with him. His was a work that included people coming and going. Mine was much more one of people coming and staying.

Up until this point, I had always viewed "chaplaincy" through the lenses of prison ministry. For the last thirteen years I, along with a great team of ministry colleagues, had centered my efforts on bringing Christ to those with abusive, abandoned, addictive, and broken backgrounds—men and women void of Hope. Most had many years of physical incarceration ahead of them.

But I never expected that I might someday benefit from a chaplaincy ministry. My experiences with chaplaincy to this point had always been centered on the needs of others. But those thoughts were now beginning to change as I sat by Darla's bedside. Hour after hour, minute by minute, I wondered what might come whenever Darla was "lifted' out of her comatose state. Now, Debbie and I were the ones in a dark place, and we desperately needed someone to empathize with our situation.

Chaplain Mark was consistent, attentive, prayerful, full of God's Word, and always hopeful. He carried the grace of Christ on his countenance. He extended a hand of Hope. He touched and spoke to Darla, even when she was totally unresponsive. He listened intently to our concerns, drew out our pain, and poured the soothing ointment of God's love over our wounds. His smile and words of genuine encouragement were like gentle afternoon showers on a parched summer garden.

After requesting our permission to pray with us, he would bring our Darla, our family, and our doctors to the throne of God. He then left us there for God's will to be done. As he gave his blessing and said his goodbyes, he always promised to stop by again before walking out the door to continue his rounds. I was left with the impression that Jesus had just passed by.

For a moment, a Peace had come over us. Our burden felt lighter. The sun peeking through the window seemed a bit more radiant. Our strength was lifted. Our situation felt bearable. But Darla was still lying there, lifeless and silent, sleeping a deep sleep. The machine was still pumping oxygen, lights were still blinking, monitors were still beeping, and nurses and doctors continued to scurry about the PICU unit.

11. Glimpses of Goodness

I have been telling people lately how thankful I am for the many blessings God has poured into my life at this time. I can feel the energy that gratefulness creates the more I live in thankfulness. It is like the constant sense of awe as when a child receives an extraordinary gift.

Journal, 2007

From the outset of our final hospital experience with Darla, Debbie and I sensed that we were going to have to cling to some kind of lifeline. We needed something we could remind each other of as we began each day, as we walked across the street and into the hospital, as we greeted Darla in her ever-worsening state, as we eagerly waited for the daily medical update on Darla. We needed a simple truth to carry us from moment to moment. We were both life-time Christians, but what we were facing was like nothing we'd ever experienced.

In what can only be attributed to our loving Father and His care over us at this time, a thought began to take a prominent place in our thinking. It went something like this: **"No matter what happens today, God is good."**

Somehow, as the days turned into weeks and as each piece of unexpected and disheartening news came crashing our way, this simple phrase helped us to remember that God truly was in control. And that whatever the circumstances were, and however disheartening our lot would become, there was no changing the reality of this simple Biblical truth:

For the LORD is good and his love endures forever;
his faithfulness continues through all generations.

Psalm 100:5

Certainly Debbie and I did not fully understand the implications of His goodness. But we were going to believe it to be true anyway.

As we heard the stories of other parents experiencing painful situations with their sick children, we quickly realized the richness of the blessings that were so much a part of our lives. For one, Debbie and I had both grown up in loving Christian families. It would be hard to overestimate the importance that this played in our ability to face the challenges that life was throwing at us. Additionally, we'd both been nurtured in grace-filled church communities from childhood to the present.

Our home church, Grace Fellowship in Atmore, was exemplary in the way it had surrounded our family with special care during some very difficult seasons. We'd started attending Grace shortly after its inception. Darla was just an infant, but was showing signs of struggle. The level of care that we received went above and beyond what we could have imagined.

Examples include coming home from hospital stays to find our yard mowed or house cleaned. Brought-in meals were common. Many sacrificially took care of our three older children during times when Debbie and I were away attending to Darla's health challenges. For one entire year our laundry was picked up weekly and brought back a day or two later washed, dried, and neatly folded.

Even in the construction of an addition to our church, we were consulted as to what would be the most helpful in attending to Darla's personal needs while on the premises. On top of these and many more practical demonstrations of love was the constant care and concern that was shown to us as we wheeled Darla into church every Sunday.

And who could forget what would, unbeknownst to us, be Darla's last Sunday at our home church. Most in our congregation were aware that we would be taking Darla for surgery the next day. Looking back, we should have probably requested some kind of special prayer on this day, but there was plenty on our minds and neither Debbie nor I had thought that far ahead to say something to our pastors.

Daddy Hold

To our surprise, as the service came to a close, our assistant pastor invited us to bring Darla to the front of the church and then invited all who were interested to surround our family for special prayer. This kind of change in service is actually quite rare in our church, so it blessed us greatly to later learn that Pastor Glenn, through the prompting of his wife, and I'm sure the guiding of the Holy Spirit, had spontaneously called for this special "sending off" prayer. Little did we know that this would be the last time that most in our congregation would see Darla on this side of heaven.

Not only had we experienced the goodness of God through our family and church heritage, but we also began to notice a variety of ways in which this goodness was flowing into our lives even as we navigated the daily disappointments of our stay in Birmingham. For starters, almost immediately within the first week of our stay in Birmingham we were able to get into the Ronald McDonald House. This was a place where families of critically ill children could lodge at minimal cost during extended hospitalizations. The housing complex was one block away from the hospital, which was definitely a blessing and helped to make everyday life more bearable.

Railroad Park was another gift from God. As the days turned into weeks, Debbie and I had developed a fairly standard routine. Depending how much sleep we were able to get each night, we would start our days with a brief but invigorating walk at this park which was just several blocks away. Its meticulously decorated and well-kept grounds provided a perfect place to walk out some of the emotions that built up on a daily basis. The early morning views of the city were inspiring. And the rubber coated trails were certainly an upgrade from anything we'd ever walked on.

The excellence and compassion of the medical community was evidenced daily. In addition to Chaplain Mark, we came to know an amazing social worker. Peggy was protective, sympathetic, cheerful, positive, realistic, generous with hugs, and always encouraging. In a lot of ways, her personality reminded me of my mom. This was another reminder of the goodness of God.

Susan, one of Darla's many nurses, was also one who stood out to us as someone that God had brought into our lives as a special gift of grace during this time.

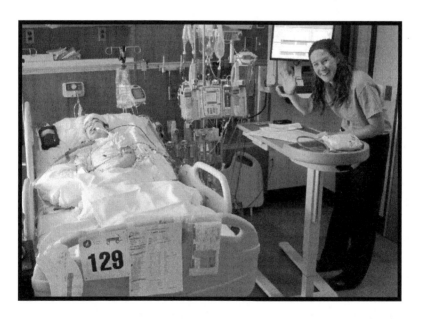

Her contagious cheerfulness and compassionate care were constant reminders that, although we were separated from all of our family and friends, God was bringing persons into our lives to stand in their places. Susan was definitely one of these special ones.

And then there was the big hospital move! In one of those days that you never forget, we were actually privileged to be a part of the "official" moving of 200 some patients from the "old" hospital we were in to a brand new nine story facility that had just been completed across the street. Not that we wanted to be a part of this move, it was just that our initial plans to be home within four or five days had been completely upended.

I thought back to our first week at the "old" hospital. Everyone was anxious and talking about the big upcoming move, and secretly in our hearts we were thinking it would be an exciting event to be a part of. Little did we know that Darla would be the first patient to occupy Room 719 in the immaculately detailed Pediatric Intensive Care Unit (PICU) of the new hospital. Stunning in the way it fit into the city's downtown landscape, the actual structure of Children's of Alabama was, in my opinion, an architectural masterpiece.

I will never forget that Saturday! It was a show of logistical expertise as "Move Teams" escorted hundreds of patients across the above-the-street glass enclosed walkway into the brand new facility. Compared to the old hospital and Intensive Care Unit, we were moving into a state-of-the-art marvel. Most notably different was our very own room with a private bath (unusual for PICU patients and their families). A wall of glass in each patient room offered breathtaking views of the city.

There were other blessings as well. Despite the everyday sadness that we were living with, Debbie and I made it a point to explore some of the unique coffee shops that existed around the city. We also found The Original Pancake House in the Five Points South section of the city to be a good place to eat a nurturing breakfast on some mornings before spending the entire day in the hospital.

But our favorite find happened while our three oldest were up for a visit well into our stay. The week had been difficult and Darla's condition was deteriorating. We felt it would be good to spend some time together as a family as a way of supporting each other in what was surely a significantly painful and personal journey for each one. Wondering where to go for supper one night, we agreed on pizza, and with the help of an iPad, Wi-Fi and some internet reviews, we landed on Johnny Brusco's Pizza in the quaint little village of Vestavia, just outside the city. The authentic New York style pizza that reminded us of our favorite pizza places going back to our Philadelphia-area roots. For those few precious moments, we enjoyed each other's company outside of the constant sadness of the hospital experience. It was definitely a gift from Above!

And then there were the cards, emails, Facebook messages, texts, and gifts from family, friends, and the community of support that God had placed around us over the years. These acts of kindness were sometimes overwhelming to us. Each expression was God's way of wrapping His loving arms around two struggling parents who were agonizing over their daughter's deteriorating condition.

Certainly, all of these "luxuries," blessings, and little surprises did not erase the deep and lingering pain that was ever growing in our hearts. After all, Darla was still imprisoned inside the four walls of a hospital room, and her condition was not looking good at all. They are memories of God's goodness that we will treasure for many years to come. But two special memories stand out above the rest.

12. The Cardboard Box

Every good and perfect gift is from above...

James 1:17a

Whereas most of our days in Birmingham felt like one piece of bad news after another, with tidal waves of despair washing over us with relentless intensity, this day was the opposite, at least in the way it began. For starters Debbie and I both "slept in" until 7 a.m., which was actually really unusual for us. Most nights one or the other of us did not sleep well. Since we awoke later than usual, we skipped our walk at Railroad Park. We wanted to stick to our normal pattern of going to the hospital as close to 8 a.m. as possible so as to be there for any new updates or visits from doctors or medical staff.

Dr. Smith, our neurologist, had been on vacation the week prior and was the first one in for a visit. We enjoyed a lengthy conversation with her, talking about everything we'd experienced with Darla in the last week. She brought us up to date on Darla's medicine levels and tried to instill some hope in us. She was fairly confident that Darla was going to "wake up." It was just taking longer than usual due to the medication levels having to be brought down from such a high dose.

While we were talking with Dr. Smith, two hospital staff persons arrived at our door pushing a cart with a nice-sized cardboard box on it. This wasn't just any cardboard box! There was quite a story behind it. For several weeks now my family in Pennsylvania had been informing me of this special box that was coming our way. There were calls to ask what kinds of snacks or items we would like; calls telling us that siblings, cousins, nieces, and nephews had gathered to bring their goodies together for packing into this box; calls to let us know that the package was on the way, and calls to see if it had arrived. Quite a number of calls were made concerning this last question, because the package never arrived, or so we thought.

You can imagine the excitement we felt knowing this special care package was on the way. We knew it would be filled with lots of love, and quite simply just knowing this box was coming had a way of giving us something to look forward to in what were some mundane and very

The Cardboard Box

discouraging times. Understandably, my oldest sister Keila became concerned when the package did not arrive within a reasonable time, so she called FedEx and tracked it down. The box had been delivered and signed for almost one week ago! The question now was "Where was it?"

Needless to say, I was becoming more and more agitated as each day passed by with no sign of the box. Several times we asked different hospital staff persons to look into it. The only answer we got was that it sometimes takes a few extra days to get something like this because of the volume of mail and packages received in a hospital complex of this size. I wasn't too sure about that response.

Eventually I became a bit more insistent, and the right person got on its trail. The box was finally discovered on the loading dock floor. We were told that since it was addressed to us (the parents) instead of Darla (the patient), it had somehow been overlooked. Let's just say that the two couriers (one of them a manager), had a look in their eyes that told me someone had messed up big-time. Unfortunately, it didn't seem that anyone wanted to take responsibility for it, and their apology reflected the same. But it really didn't matter at this point. We were happy to finally have the box in our possession.

Chaplain Mark walked in just then, and since Darla was going to another floor for an MRI, he prayed for all of us and said he'd be back later. We then proceeded to carefully unwrap this cardboard treasure box, slowly, and with much anticipation. You can't imagine the rush of excitement that this brought to us. It was like a Birthday, Anniversary, and Christmas gift all in one.

There were hand-written notes (especially touching ones from several of our little nieces), gifts for the entire family, a new blanket for Darla, and tons of snacks. Best of all were Martin's Pretzels and Herr's Cheese Curls, two of our Pennsylvania favorites! Oh, and there was Mom's custom Chex Mix too! The generosity and thoughtfulness of our family back in Pennsylvania brought tears to our eyes.

Later, Chaplain Mark walked back in and wanted to see what we got. We showed him everything, highlighting the pretzels. He said his wife loved pretzels, so we gave him one of the two bags. (He resisted, but we said "You just HAVE to try these pretzels – they are the best!")

The box wasn't the only delivery of joy on that particular day. We also received a call from home telling us we'd received a certified letter from Puerto Rico. Inside was a beautiful note of encouragement and a financial gift that left us speechless and humbled.

Threads woven through a portion of my family history reveal just how special this gift was to us and show once again the goodness of God. My father, Ray Landis, grew up in the rural village of Franconia, Pennsylvania, about an hour from Philadelphia. As was fairly common for young Mennonite adults during that time, Dad committed to several years of voluntary service. His area of service was in Puerto Rico working in the business side of operations at Aibonito Mennonite Hospital.

Part of Dad's responsibilities during his years in Puerto Rico also included assisting with several

Mennonite church plants. One of these was in a mountainous region only accessible by four-wheel drive or horseback. The young adult voluntary service team that my dad was a part of freely invited nurses from the hospital to join them for evening services in this remote mountain village. On one of these excursions a young nurse named Celia Rivera joined the group. It turned out to be a very special night. Dad preached a Gospel message, and Celia received the gift of God's grace for the very first time.

Over the coming months, a relationship developed between Ray and Celia, and they were eventually married. Dad remained in Puerto Rico for a total of nine years before returning with his young bride and two small children to the United States. I was the second born, a third was on the way, and two more would follow.

Fast forward to the spring of 2000. Debbie and I, along with my cousin Dave and his wife, Mary, attended a leadership development conference in Queens, New York where pastor and author Peter Scazzero led participants through the nuts and bolts of his groundbreaking work, Emotionally Healthy Spirituality. In one of the sessions Peter guided us through a family genogram exercise to orientate us in the area of discovering the uniqueness of our family history. At the end of the session I realized that I knew almost nothing of my mother's side. I felt at a loss.

Wanting to know more, I later called my mom and told her about this experience. Being reminded that she had an upcoming trip planned to see her family in Puerto Rico, I armed her with an outline of questions that would help me to better know this part of my family of origin. Upon her return I was delighted to go over her notes from conversations she had arranged with different relatives while on her trip.

Soon after that I received an email greeting from one of my Rivera cousins. Then, as I was just entering the world of social media at that time, I started receiving "friend" requests from more of my cousins and relatives, and little puzzle pieces of my family history began to form a beautiful picture, one that definitely became more focused during our stay in Birmingham.

It was during this time, as I wrote daily electronic updates to family and friends; I learned that a cluster of my relatives in Puerto Rico were following our story with great concern and compassion. These updates were translated into Spanish for those who did not know English well. Debbie and I were deeply touched to hear of this, and then later to learn that they were planning to take up a collection to help us with the costs of Darla's hospital stay. The letter we'd just received contained this gift.

So many people were a part of the network of support that God put around us over the years of caring for Darla that I hesitate to highlight any one in particular. But I don't think it a coincidence that the gift my Puerto Rican family gave was the exact amount needed later to cover the expenses of the beautiful memorial stone that now marks Darla's grave.

I have no doubt that God orchestrated the events surrounding The Box and The Letter to encourage our hearts that morning and prepare us for what was to come. It was only hours later that a shocking medical report would come our way.

13. Crushing News

The LORD is close to the brokenhearted
and saves those who are crushed in spirit.

Psalm 34:18

I will never forget the look in his eyes...the kind of look that makes you think that whatever is coming is going to hurt. Debbie and I were sitting on the window seat, watching the hours of another afternoon pass us by. The morning delivery and news from Puerto Rico had lifted our spirits. But something about Dr. Andrews coming into the room gave me the feeling that our morning "lift" would be short-lived.

We were always happy to see Dr. Andrews. He had

an air of professionalism mixed with compassion that we'd learned to appreciate. By this time, we'd enjoyed many conversations with him – of course about Darla – but also about life in general. I could tell this conversation was going to be different. He pulled up the closest nurse's chair and proceeded to give us the results of Darla's most recent MRI.

As only doctors can do, Dr. Andrews began to review the progression of thought that had led us from surgery number one to surgery number two. Surgery one was a devastating blow for everyone involved. No one had expected Darla's condition to worsen. We were left with few, if any, options, but after consultation with his peers around the country, Dr. Andrews presented what he felt could be a viable solution – a partial hemispherectomy. In this radical surgical procedure, the part of the brain that is considered the source of epileptic activity is disconnected (or disabled).

In Darla's case, there were more questions than answers, but in light of her current condition (she remained in an induced comatose state as these decisions were being made) we'd readily given the doctors approval to proceed. By this point we'd put all our trust in the medical community, trusting that God would work out His purposes through the knowledge and the skills He had blessed them with.

Dr. Andrews went on to describe in detail what he thought had happened in the second surgery. As he talked, tears began to well up in his weary looking eyes. I found it hard to stay focused on what he was saying. I knew bad news was coming, and it did, like someone dropping a bomb in the middle of what was already a confusing, disappointing, and extremely exhausting experience.

Dr. Andrews explained that during the second surgery he believed one microscopic cut had nicked a vital section of Darla's midbrain (the middle section of the brain stem). This cut would leave Darla in a "brain-dead" state from which she would never recover. For the first time, Dr. Andrews brought up the possibility of having to make an end-of-life decision. Even though Debbie and I both believed this "knick" could only be allowed by the hand of a loving, good, and sovereign God, we couldn't help but be devastated, shocked, and full of grief.

Despite the downward progression of Darla's condition, and the realization that Darla would not live a long life, Debbie and I never imagined that we would someday have to consider an end-of-life decision. After all, only one month earlier we'd brought Darla to Birmingham with optimistic expectations for a better quality of life for her. We'd always held on to a thread of hope for Darla, but that thread was now broken. The news could not have been any worse.

Dr. Andrews went on to provide as many details as possible, even taking us to a computer monitor at the nurses' station to review slides of Darla's most recent MRI's. Debbie was interested in these details, but by this point it really didn't matter to me. I was just trying to keep my composure and get a handle on where we were going to go from here.

One thing we both knew. We desperately wanted to talk to Mark and Peggy. We wanted to be with the two people who had ministered to us the most profoundly in our time of deepest need. These were individuals who through their callings and experience would understand our situation and help us to work through the difficult decision-making that lay ahead of us.

Since it was already early evening when the surgeon gave us this news, he let us know that he would make sure Mark and Peggy were notified to visit us first thing the next morning. In a daze, we made our way back to our room at the Ronald McDonald House. There was nothing we could do but fall onto the double bed and sob until there was nothing left to cry out.

14. Letting Go

Let us then approach God's throne of grace
with confidence, so that we may receive mercy and find
grace to help us in our time of need.

Hebrews 4:16

The following day was organized as a day of prayer and fasting for our church and ministry families and others who wished to join. The prayer room at our home church was open throughout the day for anyone to spend time interceding on behalf of our family, particularly in light of the news we'd just been given. Prayer journal pages were filled with heartfelt cries to God for Darla and for our family.

I am convinced that the prayers of God's saints on this day were what carried us over the threshold of making our decision.

I remember that morning very well. It did not take Mark and Peggy very long to show up in our room once we'd arrived, almost like they were waiting for us. As I'm sure they had done many times before in similar situations, they simply allowed us to let our tears flow in their presence—whatever tears were left after a very long night. They remained with us as long as we needed them that morning—listening, caring, praying, and simply sharing with us in Christian fellowship. It did not seem that they had anywhere else to go on this day, though I'm sure they had plenty of other things to do and patients and families to visit. Truly, Mark and Peggy were a gift from God.

But this day held other blessings as well. Over the course of our stay in Birmingham we'd received a generous number of visitors, despite the fact that we were 3 ½ hours from our home. There was no doubt that God was surrounding us with His love through these visits, despite the fact that at times our emotions were such that we could handle only brief conversations or limited contact with the "outside" world.

On this day, Calvin and Mary Jane, our "Alabama grandparents," and Dr. Jon, our family doctor, were coming to visit with us. It was no accident that Dr. Jon was along, only the grace of God. Only three years earlier Dr. Jon had faced a similar decision when his own dear wife was lying in a brain dead state after being struck by lightning. So he knew exactly what we were facing.

Debbie and I were eager for Dr. Jon to assess Darla's condition. If anyone knew Darla well, it was Dr. Jon. He had been Darla's doctor since birth and was intimately involved with our journey over the years. We were neighbors, friends, part of the same church network, and now bonded by tragic life experiences.

We made our way up from the visiting area to Darla's room, at which point Dr. Jon sensitively and lovingly assessed Darla's condition. In his own gentle way, and without really telling us what to do, he helped us to see and understand what Dr. Andrews had already tried to convey. Darla was not coming back.

After Calvin and Mary Jane and Dr. Jon left to return to Atmore, Debbie and I spent some hours alone in the room with Darla wrestling with the thought of having to make this decision. There was no way around it. We were the only ones who had the legal right to make this decision on behalf of Darla. No one else could do it for us, not even the doctors. In fact, we were nearing a point where additional invasive procedures would need to be done to prepare Darla's body for the next stage of life-extending care.

Here again I have to marvel at the way God was working "behind-the-scenes." I still can't explain why in the last half year I had bought a book titled "The Art of Dying." I love to read, and am always on the lookout for books that will stretch me in new ways, and this one fit the criteria. My curiosity in the title had nothing to do with Darla, but more to do with my own thinking about life purpose and legacy.

In the book, author Rob Moll explores the subjects of death and dying, not only through interviews and research but also through his own experience as a volunteer hospice worker. He makes the case that we will only die well if we have lived well. He shares his struggle with our culture's tendency to partition off the subject of death to hospital rooms, retirement homes, and out-of-the-way cemeteries, thus separating the reality and certainty of death from our daily existence. Although at the time I read it I was in no way thinking we would ever be in this situation, I was struck by his lament over our cultures aggressive fascination with using whatever medical means are necessary to prolong life, even when quality of life would be greatly diminished.

Obviously, these "end-of-life" topics are extremely difficult and personal, and I do not want to condemn another's way of thinking through and coming to a decision on these matters. But in my spirit, and in our situation, I had a sense that "life-extension" was not something we wanted to pursue. Even more, I could sense that the magnet of Heaven was pulling, that Darla's time on this earth was coming to an end, and that her healing was imminent.

I was not rehearsing what I had learned in this book as we sat together in Room 719. But these thoughts, along with our own life experiences, my understanding of Scripture, countless spiritual conversations with mentors over the years, and the prayers of many brought us to a point of surrender. At some point in the afternoon, we felt the peace of Christ come into the room and fill our minds. We knew that God was giving us the strength to move forward with the decision to release Darla into His eternal care.

During these moments two very special and distinct images filled our minds. Debbie, as a mother, was overtaken by the thought of God giving His own son Jesus for the sins of the world. The thought of our having to remove Darla from life support caused her to think of the pain God must have felt in allowing His son to be crucified on a rugged cross. Perhaps what hit home was the fact that Jesus was a healthy 33-year-old-man who in obedience to His Father willingly gave himself up to a brutal and violent death. In contrast, Darla, whose soul was wrapped in a body ravaged by sickness and void of any life-giving power, would only benefit by being released into her Father's loving arms.

Very rarely will anyone die for a righteous person,
though for a good person
someone might possibly dare to die.

But God demonstrates his own love for us in this:
While we were still sinners, Christ died for us.

Romans 5:7-8

Those loving arms came to my mind as well, only in a different way. For years now as the father of a special needs daughter, I had been struggling with the fact that I would never have the opportunity to walk my precious daughter down the aisle of matrimony. It was not until this particular afternoon, as we were wrestling with what to do, that I believe God gave me a picture to settle my wounded spirit and help me cross over the threshold of this decision. In my mind, I was impressed with the idea that by choosing to remove Darla from life support, I was being given the unique opportunity and special privilege of ushering my youngest daughter "down the aisle" to an eternal Groom like no other, the Lord Jesus Christ! From the standpoint of a father, could there really ever be a better passing over from one life to the next?

I would soon know the pain and glory of that hand-off.

15. A Most Difficult Conversation

My soul is weary with sorrow;
strengthen me according to your word.

Psalm 119:28

Once Debbie and I had made this decision, we knew that the first thing we wanted to do was notify our children and our parents. We didn't want to have this conversation with our children over the phone, so we decided the next best thing would be to schedule a video meeting over the internet.

As mentioned earlier, one of the most difficult parts of our experience in Birmingham was the three and one-half hours that separated us from Diana, David, and Darren, as well as the many close friends we'd in our hometown of Atmore. We'd grown accustomed to not having immediate family around, having lived a thousand miles away from parents and siblings for over a decade. Obviously, there were many times when we wished we could have been together. This was definitely one of those times.

Fortunately, with the help of modern technology, we were able to stay in contact with friends and relatives across the miles as much as we wanted to. And many times a text, Facebook message, or phone call provided the encouragement that was needed to help us get through one more day. But the video conference call to inform our children of our decision to remove their sister from life support will stand out as one of the all-time most difficult things I have ever had to do.

Debbie's parents had flown down the weekend before to visit us in Birmingham and were now spending the week with our children in Atmore. That was a huge blessing, because their tangible presence with our oldest three would be desperately needed for this difficult conversation.

Debbie and I situated ourselves on the edge of the bed in our room at the Ronald McDonald House, our laptop on the night stand facing us. How in the world was I going to break this news? How should I say what needed to be said? Would I be able to keep my composure? All I could think of was to dial in to our kids at the scheduled time and trust that God would give me the right words to say. And He did.

One thing we'd really learned to appreciate in these years of constant communication with the medical community was to be told exactly what was going on without holding anything back. In other words, "Just say what needs to be said!" Obviously, that is not always an easy task, and this was certainly one of those situations. But it's what I was going to attempt to do – with as much grace and love as I could muster within myself. Debbie and I looked into the laptop screen. There they were, sitting on the sofa in our family room, 200 road miles apart from us. Diana, David, Darren, and Nana and Pop Pop Kulp. I explained the details that we'd learned a day earlier and how we'd come to our decision. In just two days, we would surround Darla as a family and usher her Home.

Our family was stunned. You would think that after years of hardship for Darla the thought of her going home to be with Jesus would bring a sense of relief. In some under-the-surface way, I think that feeling was there in all of us, but this was no time for thinking in those terms. This was going to be a tremendous loss for us.

I encouraged the children to allow themselves to cry, if not now, then on their pillows when they went to bed. Naturally, there were tears of various intensities on both sides of the screen, and I'm sure there were some on their pillows later too. I know there were on ours. Debbie and I were so glad that her parents were at the house standing in the gap for us. Their support for our children was priceless in these moments.

With the news-breaking call behind us, and a dreaded appointment with death before us, we settled in for the night, completely exhausted. We hoped that the night ahead would kindly give us at least a few hours of sleep. Tomorrow would be a day of preparation. The following day would be our last in Birmingham.

16. Not Just Another Day

Why, you do not even know what will happen
tomorrow. What is your life? You are a mist that
appears for a little while and then vanishes.

James 4:14

Though everything about our morning routine
was familiar by now, this day didn't "feel" the
same. We knew what was to come would be
extremely difficult, but there was no way we could
fathom the sharpness of the pain we would soon feel.
How does one even prepare for what would no doubt be
a life-defining experience?

We started this, our 32nd and final day in
Birmingham, with a morning walk around Railroad

Park. There wasn't really "extra" time to make a second loop, so we walked the few blocks back to our room, quickly showered, and selected nicer than usual outfits out of our luggage to wear for this "special" day. After all, family members were on their way to join us for Darla's homegoing.

We headed out the door, across the street, and over one city block towards the front entrance of the hospital.

Hand-in-hand, we walked through the automatic sliding doors and into the hugely expansive and awe-inspiring foyer. Bypassing the elevator to the first floor, we headed for the long flight of circular stairs up to the main reception area. (We'd prided ourselves over the last month in knowing that we were at least getting some semblance of exercise each day by going up and down this beautiful stairway every time we came in and out of the hospital.) Once on the main reception level we headed straight for the central hospital elevator platform, pushed "UP" and waited for one of the six doors to open.

In some ways I was hoping we wouldn't bump into any familiar faces. We'd gotten to know a good number of moms and dads, other visitors, and medical and hospital staff – some of whom by this point had become like comrades in a battle for life. Right or wrong, I felt like I needed to remain composed, and seeing someone we knew could tip me over the emotional scale. I really didn't feel like crying in front of anybody just yet, figuring there was plenty of that to come.

Upon arriving on the 7th floor, we navigated the now familiar remaining hallways, arrived at the entrance to the PICU, and waited for the clearance buzzer before pushing the doors open. Once inside, we rounded one more corner and passed a half a dozen rooms before arriving at the doorway to 719.

Darla looked about the same as she had for the last several weeks, a motionless body surrounded by life supporting equipment. There were lines, hoses, lights, beeping, liquids, doctors, nurses, comings, goings, charts, monitors, and so much more. As far as I was concerned, it was all just a big blur today. But like we did each and every day, we immediately went to Darla's side, talked to her and touched her, and wondered how all of this could be.

A myriad of thoughts and memories were swirling through our minds. Only about twelve hours earlier we'd walked to the end of the hallway of the 7th floor PICU unit and stood in front of the wall of windows overlooking the west side of the city. The sun was lowering itself into the horizon in a brilliant display of orange mixed with a deep dusk blue. We just stood there and watched. Awed, but conflicted. How could this kind of beauty be intermixed with so much grief all at the same time? How could it be that this would be Darla's last sunset? The only consolation that came to my mind was that the sun was only setting. It would rise again on the other side as a brand new day for Darla, and for us.

Not long after we'd settled ourselves in the room, Peggy arrived. We couldn't have been more grateful to receive her morning greeting and customary hugs.

On this, our last day, Peggy was like a mama bear with her cubs. She knew this would probably be the most difficult day we'd ever experienced. She was determined to do everything she could to direct the flow of traffic in and out of our room and see to it that every conceivable need or desire was attended to. There were few moments throughout this day when we did not sense her presence. Her affection was such that it will never be forgotten.

17. A Mother's Love

...whoever wants to become great among you
must be your servant, and whoever wants to be first
must be your slave – just as the Son of Man did not
come to be served, but to serve,
and to give his life as a ransom for many.

Matthew 20:26-28

There was one thing that Debbie and I knew we wanted to do before the family arrived, and that was to hold Darla one last time. This was a fairly complicated task considering the amount of life-supporting lines she was connected to. Peggy went right to work and tracked down several nurses who could help us. They set about arranging the room to accommodate us with this and removing as many of the lines as possible. I then helped one of the nurses to lift Darla's lifeless body into Debbie's arms, after which they all left the room to give us some privacy. Tears flowed as we took in these moments, but mostly we hoped that somehow in this final act of tenderness Darla would understand our deep love for her. Maybe even "feel" our love through the haze of her condition.

A Mother's Love

Inside, my heart was breaking as I sat next to Debbie and Darla. I could not imagine the wrenching pain that must have been going through Debbie's heart as a mother. What I did know with certainty was that for almost thirteen years I had witnessed first-hand one of the most amazing displays of God's grace that I will ever know. I cannot even remember one instance where Debbie complained about Darla's situation. Struggled, yes, but if there was ever a complaint, it would have been totally uncharacteristic of what was the norm.

Time after time I was humbled to watch the care and attention Debbie gave to Darla, and all of it with a level of patience I knew little about. Meticulously dressed and attended to, Darla was obviously treated as the most honored member of our family by her mother. A note from one of the many cards received after Darla's death communicated Debbie's care for Darla this way:

> *I will never forget the impression your loving care for Darla had on me the first time I met you. She was the gentlest, sweetest, and prettiest child. I enjoyed the opportunity to care for her in Moppets [the childcare portion of a MOPS (Mothers of Preschoolers) meeting] one morning and remember thinking how well cared for and loved she was just from observing her neatly groomed hair, cute clothes, and calm, gentle demeanor.*

So for me to watch this heartbreaking scene of a mother holding her much loved child for the very last time was almost more than I could bear.

I suppose one never really knows what is the right amount of time for moments like this to continue. On the one hand, we knew what was coming and longed for

Daddy Hold

a sense of glorious finality to what had been an extremely painful journey for Darla. On the other hand, we knew that these moments would never be repeated again.

After a while, Debbie let me know that she was ready to hand Darla over to me. I went out and told the nurses we were ready to make a switch. Soon they came back and re-arranged everything for me to hold Darla. Although it was the most awkward of circumstances...tubes and lines connecting Darla to the machines that were keeping her alive...it was also the "Daddy Hold" that I will always remember most. I guess you could say it was the hold of a lifetime.

18. Daddy Hold

There is still an underlying desire for recognition in my
life. I wonder if, as a leader, that ever goes away. I pray
that it is not what it used to be, but I'm afraid it's still
there disguised in other ways.

It seems the path to servanthood is through acts of
service. Continual. Day by day. I feel that happening
some with taking care of Darla.

Journal, 2010

"D addy Hold" had become a well-used
term at our house over the years.
Darla loved to be held by her Daddy,
and Daddy loved to hold his Darla. It was at least a
daily occurrence, often more than once. Many times

when I got home from work at the end of the day I was welcomed by Darla. She would know that I had arrived and start following me with her eyes. I knew she wanted me to hold her, and she knew that if she kept her eyes on me, I would not be able to resist her for long – especially if she started to raise her hands and her arms toward me.

I'm not sure who benefitted the most – Daddy or Darla. I know Darla, even at twelve years of age, enjoyed being held. She would snuggle into just the right position, a faint smile would cross over her baby-skinned face, and more often than not, she would simply fall asleep. No one can know how much I treasured

those moments. Sometimes I fell asleep myself.

But in the strangest way it was also good for me. Holding Darla had a way of helping me to keep things in perspective. It seemed that no matter what was going on at the time, a "Daddy Hold" would take care of what was ailing me. In fact, it became known around our house, at least by my wife, that if Daddy needed to get his act straightened out, then it was time for a "Daddy Hold."

Somehow, holding Darla, looking into her face, making her smile, and thinking about her life that was racked by illness, had a way of taking me back to center, back to the important things, back to verses like: "...whatever is true, whatever is noble, whatever is right, whatever is pure, whatever is lovely, whatever is admirable – if anything is excellent or praiseworthy – think about such things." (Philippians 4:8)

Darla's life was a treasure from God. Her simple ways, visual contentment, and smile brought balance and perspective to life. Darla was a joy-giver. She helped me to discern what was important and what was not so important. She had a way of simplifying and clarifying my theological mind games. She had a way of answering my questions without saying a word. In the end, she helped me to fully grasp and appreciate the truth and meaning behind the words of her favorite song.

> Jesus loves me! This I know,
> For the Bible tells me so;
> Little ones to Him belong,
> They are weak but He is strong.[4]

---

[4] Anna Bartlett Warner, 1859

Daddy Hold

So, on this particular Friday, the day we knew would be her last, I held Darla one more time. And while I was holding her, all I could think about was that for almost 13 years I had been given the most precious of gifts. A

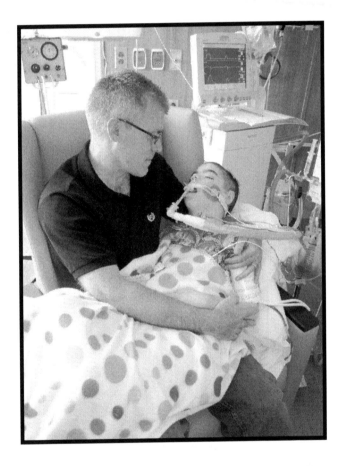

very special child who needed to be held was given to a very needy Dad who loved to hold her. You would think I would have spent most of that time crying. Instead, it was like playing a fast forward movie of all the "Daddy

Holds" I had been able to experience over the years. My heart overflowed with thanksgiving toward God. This time, I was the one with the faint smile creeping across my face.

At some point, we knew it was time to move on, so we called the nurses in to help us place Darla back in her bed and reconnect her with all of the lines. Then we went over to the window and sat together in silence. These would be our last few quiet moments just the two of us together with Darla. The pain inside was almost unbearable. Knowing that our family would soon be arriving offered temporary comfort, enough to push us through the fog of our conflicting emotions. Before long, we received a text or a phone call letting us know that the first of our guests had arrived.

19. A Final Gathering

Love never gives up, never loses faith, is always hopeful,
and endures through every circumstance.

1 Corinthians 13:7 (NLT)

Our three oldest, along with Debbie's parents, Nana and Pop Pop Kulp, and our "Alabama grandparents," Calvin and Mary Jane Schrock, arrived together at noon. Debbie and I went down to the 2nd floor entrance area to meet them. Diana immediately showed us a hat that she had crocheted for Darla to wear for her homegoing. I couldn't help but choke back tears.

Within a short time our pastor, Gene King, and his

wife Judy arrived. Mom and my brother, Alvin, arrived a few minutes later. They had flown down from Pennsylvania just that morning. (We'd found out they were coming less than 24 hours before, and it was truly a blessing to have some of my own family members with us for what would only be a few hours.) There were lots of tears and hugs with everybody in those moments. Each of these represented "family" to us, and if there was ever a time we needed support, it was now.

After the initial greetings, we helped everyone to get registered and signed in as guests, and made our way up to the 7th floor. A visiting room had been reserved for our family to use as a private gathering place throughout the day. We walked down the hallway as a group, filed into the private waiting room and collectively set our hearts to the reality that awaited us. It was time for our final visits with Darla to begin.

Debbie and I felt that it would be best to go in with the children first. My expectation was that, other than the actual act of removing Darla from life support, this would be the most difficult part of the day. We would be saying our final goodbyes to a daughter and a sister, one who had profoundly impacted our family experience.

I can't think of anything in life that would actually prepare a family for a moment like this. We'd tried to be open with the older three over the years about the fact that Darla would likely not live a "full" life in the way that most do, but we'd never thought about or talked about the fact that we might someday have to remove Darla from life support.

Leaving our supporting umbrella of care behind, Debbie, I, and the children began the lonely walk down the hallway towards Room 719. As we entered Darla's room, the stark realization hit me that these would be our last moments together as a family of six. Our hearts were filled with the richness of wonderful memories with Darla. Yet at the same time each of us was in somewhat of a daze as to what we were about to experience. You can't imagine how excruciatingly painful these moments were to me as a father, but I tried my best to keep some sense of composure to help "carry" my family, as it were, through these moments.

Debbie and Diana immediately began to work at carefully putting Darla's new hat on. It would be a fitting covering for her recently shaved head and the

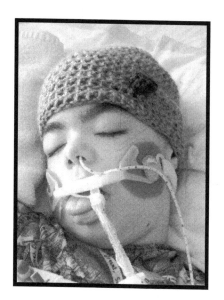

painful looking surgery scars that wrapped around her skull. The hat was grey, with a burgundy flower, and looked beautiful on Darla.

It was not unlike Diana to do something like this. She loved her sister very much, having shared a bedroom for all of Darla's life. When I say "shared a bedroom," I am not talking about what most of us would think who might have also shared a bedroom with a sibling. There were many times when it probably felt more like a hospital room. Darla had many of her seizures while in her bed, and there was always someone coming to check on her, give her medicine, lift her onto her changing table, or any number of other things associated with the day-by-day care of a special needs child.

In fact, many of those caring moments were given by Diana herself. It was not uncommon to see Diana holding Darla, maybe reading or singing lightly to her, but usually just holding. And you could easily see that

Darla was just as content as could be. In many ways Diana was like a second mother to Darla, so for her to crochet this little hat for Darla to wear for the last few hours of her life was a very special gesture.

Darla's brothers also had a special love for her with each of them expressing it in different ways. David's was more practical. One story that stands out came from someone at church. In a group discussion where David was present, the question was asked, "What would you do if you won one million dollars?" David's immediate response was that he would use it to pay for past or future medical care and expenses relating to Darla. I think our entire family would have shared that sentiment as well. David was also especially helpful to his mother. He looked out for her by regularly checking with her to make sure she was doing ok with the heavy load of care that she was responsible for.

Darren's way of caring centered more on how Darla was feeling each day. If she was not doing well, his

compassionate side would kick in, and he would find a way to encourage her by gently speaking to or touching her. Sometimes he wanted to just sit next to her on the sofa.

One thing was sure. Each family member had their own way of helping out over the years, and I have no doubt that their worldviews, character, and general outlook on life was and will be significantly impacted by

having had a sister like Darla. I wish I could say we always had mature views on how to love and accept a special needs sister and daughter. I know there were times we could have handled things differently. But like anything else, our acceptance of who Darla was and the way that we cared for her were all formed in the crucible of experiences.

In that hospital room, in those final and most precious minutes together, those experiences were all a part of the thoughts and questions that were going through our minds. Although we didn't talk about it in those moments, I have to wonder if all of us wanted to ask the same basic question, "Why?"

It was during our final family moments that Darla's neurologist stopped in to say her last goodbyes. She was the one who had initially encouraged us to move forward with surgery. She was also the one who now seemed to resist our decision the most...not in a disrespectful way, but in the sense that she could hardly believe her "plan" did not work. To be honest, it was hard for us to believe we were at this point too.

So as we stood around Darla's bedside, it was understandable that Dr. Smith was deeply troubled and greatly disappointed. She, Dr. Andrews, and the entire medical team had been optimistic that Darla was going to see at least some improvement. Through conversations over the last day or two, we'd gently tried to explain to Dr. Smith why we felt it was time for Darla to go Home. She was not ready to give up, as it were. Perhaps with more time improvement would come, she felt.

However, by this point we were convinced otherwise, so as we'd already done, again we let Dr. Smith know that we were freeing her, as a doctor, from the responsibility of Darla's care. We assured her that we felt no bitterness, and offered our forgiveness in case it was needed. With tears in her eyes, she hugged Debbie and I, and then slowly walked out of the room.

Daddy Hold

What else is there to do in these final moments as a family? A part of me wanted to savor this time forever, but the reality was that it was getting closer to the time when we would have to say our final goodbyes. With more tears, more hugs, and a final family prayer, we circled around Darla's bedside. We thanked God for her

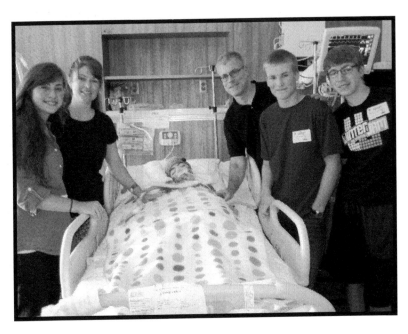

short but profoundly impactful life. We asked God to be merciful in Darla's dying moments. Then as a family we released her to the One who could bring the healing we'd prayed for all of these years.

Of course, there was a final family picture too, though we all looked quite red-eyed, to say the least.

By this point we were ready to invite our extended family into 719. So Debbie's parents, my mom, and my brother, Alvin, joined us. Again, there were tears and hugs. Deep emotion filled the room. We began to get the sense that we were on the verge of a holy experience. After about 15 or 20 minutes we invited our remaining guests into the room. As we gathered around Darla's bedside, everyone began to talk and relax just a bit. Different ones shared memories of Darla.

Pastor Gene remembered the high pitched squeal Darla would make during Sunday worship. He said he always thought she was praying or singing or shouting "Amen." He considered it to be Darla's expression of worship and joy.

Other memories were shared too, all of which were helpful and good for these moments. But we all knew that our time with Darla was coming to an end, so as a group we closed in around Darla one more time for Pastor Gene to lead us in a prayer. Once again, we asked God for mercy and released Darla into His eternal care. As we finished praying, one of Darla's PICU floor doctors came in and helped to lighten things up a bit, if that were possible. Her presence was a blessing, as her expertise had been in the weeks prior.

Earlier, we'd arranged for Dr. Andrews, Darla's surgeon, to come in and greet the family. He was running a bit behind, and to be honest, the waiting was getting a bit awkward. We all kind of breathed a sigh of relief when he finally arrived. Debbie and I had gotten to know Dr. Andrews quite well by this time. We'd engaged in quite a few conversations with him about Darla's care, including end-of-life issues. We'd grown to respect him greatly and appreciated the intense concern he had demonstrated towards Darla throughout our 32 days in Birmingham.

Daddy Hold

After we introduced everyone in the room to Dr. Andrews, he went on to share a bit of his reflections on the last month. Pre-surgery discussions were all filled with hopeful dialogue. He had no reason to believe that after 80+ "successful" callosotomies (the first surgery) Darla's condition couldn't be improved – at least to some degree.

But it was not meant to be. Darla's course took a much different direction than anyone could have imagined. Hers was the only callosotomy of his that had "backfired" like this. As he had explained it to us earlier, the first surgery seemed to unlock something in Darla's brain. Instead of fewer seizures, there were more. Many more. He said it was like someone had lit a match and thrown it onto a dry forest bed.

Dr. Andrews felt so terribly sorry for the way things had turned out, but we knew that it was through his tireless efforts that we were able to come to a peace that we as parents had done everything that was humanly possible to help our struggling daughter. On behalf of those gathered with us, I thanked Dr. Andrews for his courageous efforts in the last month. Debbie and I both knew he had exhausted every source of knowledge he could get hold of. We knew he had spent many of his evening hours seeking counsel on Darla's situation from medical associates across the country.

We were coming to the end of a long journey. Every option had now been exhausted. Now it was time to release our daughter into the arms of the only One who could bring complete healing to her now weakened and lifeless body. With our family and friends as an audience, we released Dr. Andrews from Darla's care and told him, as we'd told other doctors, that we held no bitterness or unforgiveness in our hearts towards him. Debbie hugged and thanked him, I did the same, and he walked out of the room.

20. Holy Ground

Your eyes saw my unformed body;
all the days ordained for me were written in your book
before one of them came to be.

Psalm 139:16

The day before, Debbie and I had received a visit from the Palliative Care Team. This group is trained to assist with situations that involve suffering and death. They explained to us the possible scenarios we could face once Darla's life support was removed. Their explanation was sobering, but helpful, and we thought that David, Diana, and Darren, at least, would benefit from knowing more detail about what could happen after removing the life support systems. It was decided in that meeting that they would go through their explanation with those who had come to witness Darla's homegoing. When we were ready, we paged the PC Team and gathered again in the private visitation room to hear their explanation and prepare ourselves for the thing we all dreaded.

The PC Team explained the process and the three possible scenarios. Once life support was removed, a person could pass away within 1) minutes, 2) hours or days, or 3) days or weeks. They predicted that Darla would be in the second or third category. That prediction messed with my mind quite a bit, but Debbie had a growing sense that it would not be a long process. In a God-given and informative conversation with Darla's respiratory therapist the night before, Debbie became convinced and at rest that Darla would pass away sooner rather than later.

We gave everyone the choice as to whether they wanted to be in the room at the exact time of Darla's support being removed. Our boys decided to stay out. Calvin and Mary Jane would stay with them. Someone would go and get them later, if and when it looked like the difficulty of waiting was coming to an end. Those of us who wanted to be there from the outset made our way to Room 719. It was time.

It did not take long for the medical team to set things in motion. Within minutes they were gathered around Darla, gently removing the breathing tube that had kept her alive for the last three weeks. I did not watch them pull it out. But as soon as I knew they were done, I looked over, and I saw that Darla's skin color was turning shades of grey and blue. I was not expecting that, at least not so soon. I was not sure what it meant, but I got this sense that Darla's life was very near to an end.

I immediately went over and started talking to Darla. Debbie was right with her – one hand on her heart. I put my face to Darla's and told her that she could go Home – that it was OK. I kept saying that to her, not able to pull myself away. I pushed my chin into the pillow next to her face. We were cheek to cheek. Debbie was inches away on the other side. Darla was on her way Home – and we as parents were right there with her, surrounded by loving family support. By this point, everyone in the room was crying, at least to some degree.

Within minutes, it appeared that Darla had stopped breathing so I asked Pastor Gene to go and get the boys and Calvin and Mary Jane. Debbie kept her hand on Darla's heart the whole time, waiting for the beating to come to an end. I kept looking at her, expecting her to give me an indication of Darla's last heartbeat. Minutes later, the lead doctor came over, held Darla's hand, looked us in the eye, and left the room. Darla was gone. It was 2:30 p.m. All of this had happened in less than 15 minutes.

I can't tell you the feelings and emotions that accompanied those last moments for me. They are too deep and too complex. But in the seconds that followed, as we stood by Darla's side, I put my arms tightly around the shoulders of David and Darren, looked upward, and loudly cried out "Thank You, Jesus!"

Then I said it again, because I felt we'd just witnessed a miracle. We'd just been given a gift.

Unfortunately, it was hard to envision what this healing might look like as we all stared at Darla's lifeless body. But I can assure you that in the minutes surrounding Darla's passing from one side to the other there was a certain clarity about life. In these special moments the focus was so sharp I almost wished I could have put some in a bottle. There was very little that seemed important, critical, or urgent at this point - only faith, hope and love. And if you just wanted to boil it down to one thing, it would be love. (1 Cor. 13:13)

Despite deep emotions, everyone in the room comforted each other with the fact that our prayers for a quick and painless transition for Darla had been answered. God had been merciful. Our Darla was finally with Jesus, safely Home in that place we all long for. She was healed at last from the seizures that had plagued her for most of her short life.

Once we felt like the appropriate grieving for this moment was over, everyone except Debbie and me left the room. After helping the nurse to freshen and wrap up Darla's body, Debbie held Darla one last time. I do not remember how long this was, and it really didn't matter. These are once-in-a-lifetime moments that can never be recovered. Needless to say there was a solemnity about these moments—a tremendous finality about what had just happened. It would take more time for reality set in. But one thing was sure. Our hearts were broken and hurting.

At some point, experiences like this come to an end. You want to stay, but you also know it's time to go. Debbie and I both kissed Darla on her cheeks and forehead one more time. Then we walked out of the room and closed the door most of the way. I say most of the way because the last image I have of Darla is looking back through the gap in the almost closed door. Her body, drained of warmth, was lying on the bed. But I knew she was Home… safely Home… away from the body and at home with the Lord. (2 Corinthians 5:8b)

We walked down the hallway to rejoin the rest of our family. There were still bags to pack, a room to clean, flights for family members to catch, and a 3 ½ hour ride back to our home in Atmore. It was only mid-afternoon, but already felt like a very long day.

Some, I suppose, would say it was a bad day. I agree that it was very difficult and extremely sorrowful. We'd lost a precious daughter, sister, and granddaughter. Yet in so many ways, as I reflected on the goodness of God during our 32 days in Birmingham, and now on the happenings of this, our last day with Darla, I also have to say that it was a "good" day. Because in the midst of the pain there was Hope. A Hope that was eternal. A Hope that would never die. A Hope that can only be found through Jesus Christ.

We chose to take one more opportunity to savor the goodness of God before the long drive back to our home. Though in some ways it felt awkward to enjoy anything at this point, we, along with our remaining three children, agreed that it would be good to stop for supper on our way out of the city. And there was no question that the place would be Johnny Brusco's Pizza.

Daddy Hold

I had a dream about Darla. We did not speak to each other. We did not sit together as we used to do. She didn't hold my hand, nor did I run my fingers through her hair or call her "Pretty Girl" as I often did.

But I did see her running through a field of daisies with her arms stretched out, with long flowing hair and sunshine on her face, smiling and being just the sweet Darla Joy she has always been.

Lord, how I long to run with her.

Jose Morales (Darla's friend)

21. The Silent Missionary

But God chose the foolish things of the world
to shame the wise; God chose the weak things of the
world to shame the strong. God chose the lowly things
of this world and the despised things – and the things
that are not – to nullify the things that are,
so that no one may boast before him.

1 Corinthians 1:27-29

D uring our time in Birmingham my mom began to call Darla the "Silent Missionary" because of the way her life story was reaching across the miles through electronic prayer networking and social media. She touched hearts in ways we do not yet comprehend. Her reach went farther than many who live a full life. She was a silent but booming witness to the power of Christ's love through weakness. Perhaps this is what Paul is speaking about in his letter to the Corinthian believers

when he writes "God chose the weak things of the world to shame the strong." (1 Corinthians 1:27b)

Strength through weakness is a concept that can easily be lost. I have noticed that one of the greatest dangers faced by those of us who serve in any kind of ministry is that we put ourselves in a category that is "above" those we are serving. This is unfortunate and damaging. If we are not careful, we can adopt an "us" versus "them" mentality. We have the answers. They have the questions. We have the solutions. They have the problems. We have the resources. They have the needs and special challenges. We are looking down at them. They are looking up to us. We are doing fine. They are not.

Perhaps that is why some of us struggle with besetting sins, or go through seasons of drought, or carry heavy burdens allowed by our Father. In these darker moments we are more prone to readily acknowledge our need for grace. And in that awareness we may be more likely to extend it to others.

It seems that in order for anyone to be able to effectively reach out to and love what we would consider the "least of these," we have to ourselves become, or at least put ourselves in the place of those who are least. We must acknowledge our own neediness and open ourselves to receive grace rather than thinking we have something to prove by displaying a strength we don't even possess.

In the business world we climb over each other to make it to the top. In church life we elevate those who have talent and charisma. In our educational systems we honor the intelligent and worship the athletic. In sports we bankroll empires of power and dominance through our obsessions with superstars and dynasties.

Where in all of this is there room for the lowly, the abandoned, the marginalized, the neglected, the silenced, and the forgotten? How can we show respect for God's image in the truest sense? How can we live and operate within this culture of superiority yet understand that the way of the Jesus Kingdom is one that takes us downward, backward, underneath, rock bottom, behind, and under cover?

Darla's life was a constant and gut-wrenching reminder to me of the necessity to love and care for the down-and-outer in our midst, especially those with no power and no voice. She helped me to see the preciousness of each child of God.

In his book, "The Life You've Always Wanted", Author and Pastor John Ortberg suggests that we enter a life of servanthood through the "Ministry of the Mundane." He writes:

Jesus took a little child in his arms and said, in effect, "Here's your ministry. Give yourselves to those who can bring you no status or clout. Just help people. You need this little child. You need to help this little child, not just for her sake, but more for your sake. For if you don't, your whole life will be thrown away on an idiotic contest to see who is the greatest. But if you serve her – often and well and cheerfully and out of the limelight – then the day may come when you do it without thinking, 'What a wonderful thing I've done.' Then you will begin serving naturally, effortlessly, for the joy of it. Then you will begin to understand how life in the kingdom works.[5]

---

[5] John Ortberg, *The Life You've Always Wanted: Spiritual Disciplines for Ordinary People* (Grand Rapids: Zondervan, 2002), 118.

It is true that some now consider us "blessed" to be relieved of the burden of caring for a special needs child, and I suppose to some extent that may be true. If nothing else, Darla is in a place we long to be, and we do have much more freedom. But the truth of the matter is that Darla was a joy-giver. She brought something to the table that only she could bring. Her uniqueness was unquestionable. Her impact, eternal.

Epilogue

Dear Darla,

How long is one day in heaven? Or one year?
Who's putting braids in your hair?
How fast can you run?
Do you still like PB&J sandwiches dipped in milk?
What is your favorite color?
Who are you playing with?
Do you like to swim?
What is your favorite song?

But most of all,
what is it like to be held by the Alpha and the Omega,
the First and the Last,
the Beginning and the End,
the Root and the Offspring of David,
the Bright Morning Star,
the Lamb of God,
Jesus the Christ, the Son of the Living God?

Love, Daddy

Journal, one-year anniversary of Darla's homegoing.

Daddy Hold

It was not long after Darla's homegoing that I went to my friend's cabin in northern Georgia. (This was mentioned in the prologue.) While there, Del and his wife, Marj, invited me to go to church with them on Sunday morning – a small-town Methodist Church. I enjoyed the service very much, and was almost startled when, for the closing song, the choir sang "Jesus Loves Me, This I Know."

I thought to myself, "How often do you hear 'Jesus Loves Me' in a Sunday morning service?" I couldn't help but think of the smile this song brought to Darla's face every time she heard it. Inside, I was comforted to imagine that God was thinking of me in this very moment.

A few months later, Debbie was given the gift of a flight to Pennsylvania to spend a weekend with a close friend who was not able to attend Darla's funeral. They also went to church together on Sunday morning. Right after lunch I received a text from Debbie saying, "Can you believe it? The worship team sang Jesus Loves Me!!!" I was amazed! In my view these two occurrences were not coincidences, but rather, our very own "Daddy Hold" from our Father above.

Epilogue

There is no doubt in my mind that our joy is being restored, though I must admit it is slower in coming than I would have thought. There does not seem to be a shortcut through the grieving journey. But as time passes it does seem that I am seeing little glimpses of joy resurfacing after a long winter. I am learning to be okay with that. Life must go on, but it is clear that I am going to walk with a limp for the rest of my life.

Yet there is something about walking with a limp that also feels like a gift. There is a realization that more is needed for going on with life than I possess. Within me is a new sense of dependency. I have a longing, and a greater hope of life eternal. What strength was lost will be compensated by a new realization of joy. A restoration is in progress.

I usually called Debbie on my way into the prison to let her know that she wouldn't be able to get hold of me. It's always a nice way to "check in" with her before shifting my mind to "prison chaplain" mode. I dialed her up, as usual, for a quick chat. When she picked up the phone and we began our conversation, I noticed there was not as much "life" on the other end as I am used to.

I asked Debbie if she was home alone. She was. "That could be some of it," I thought. "Debbie is more of a people person." Since we were close to the one-year anniversary of Darla's homegoing, it would certainly be understandable for her to be reflecting on the journey of the last year. And, as we have discovered, that reflection can quickly lead to sorrow if one allows it happen.

Debbie was baking cookies. Sugar cookies. Those, I think, are my favorite, especially with a cup of coffee in the quiet morning hours. "Well, that's sweet of her," I thought, "baking my favorite cookies!" Then there was a pause on the other end. I knew what that meant. After

we both composed ourselves, she told me that her baking was reminding her of how Darla used to scoot over to the kitchen and lie on the floor mat in front of the back door. She would just lie there, content to simply be close to her Mommy as she was baking.

Our conversation held another pause or two, and some broken words. Then the thought came to me that this was actually a good memory. A sweet memory. And that, I knew, was an answer to many prayers. For what had seemed like a very long time, we'd found it very difficult to move past the images of Darla lying in a hospital bed with her eyes closed. There were other images too. Ones I guess in some way I wish we could forget. Now, finally, this mental picture of Darla lying on the floor mat in the kitchen came as a refreshing wind. Thanksgiving welled up inside of me, for though simple and seemingly long in coming, this memory was a blessing that I was going to name, and count.

We finished our conversation as I drove up to the prison and parked my car. I took a deep breath, wiped the wetness from around my eyes, gathered my books and things, and headed for the gated entrance. It turned out to be what I would consider an "average" afternoon in the prison. Nothing stood out one way or the other. But when I finished for the day, left the prison, and returned to my office at We Care, I found a zip-lock bag filled with sugar cookies on my desk. On the outside of the bag, written in red, were the words, "I love u."

Of course there were, and continue to be, many other "little stories" of God's grace being evidenced in our lives as we emerged from what was a season of significant loss. Yet inside there was a growing sense that there was one more journey that we would need to take.

Daddy Hold

I am not sure when I first mentioned this idea to Debbie, but at some point we began to talk about arranging a meeting with Darla's medical team around the one-year mark of her passing. Even though our time at Children's will always stand out as the darkest and most painful moments that Debbie and I and our family have ever experienced, there is also the unquestionable reality that those 32 days were also a time of great focus, encouragement, and transformation. We both knew that it would be good for us to go back and say "Thank You" again, to deliver some of Debbie's home-baked goods, to reconnect with those who had become such a special part of our lives. We knew we wanted to go back for a visit.

Our first step was to get in touch with Traci. She was the one who always seemed to be able to get things done when it came to appointments and problem solving during our time at Children's. She also showed a special and genuine interest in our journey with Darla, having assisted with both of the surgeries. With Traci's help, a meeting was arranged that would include Darla's surgeon and neurologist and, of course, Mark and Peggy. Naturally, Traci would be there too. In the back of our minds we were hoping that we would also get to see Nurse Susan. But we'd forgotten to mention her to Traci, so we just figured that if she was working on that day we might bump into her.

The day came and we made the 250-mile trip to Birmingham. We pulled into a parking space in the parking garage, turned off the engine, and just sat there for a few quiet moments. Breathing deeply, we gathered up the boxes of baked goods and headed across the walkway to the main reception area. We were early, so we slowly meandered across the expansive visiting area and found a place to wait, even walking down and then back up the circular stairways that had been such a part of our daily comings and goings.

Just before our scheduled meeting time Traci appeared in the elevator waiting area. It was time to return to the seventh floor—the PICU—and into a conference room that had been reserved for this special occasion. Within minutes, everyone who had been invited was present. Traci, Mark and Peggy, Dr. Smith and Dr. Andrews, and the floor doctor who had attended to Darla's homegoing. Warm greetings and hugs were exchanged.

There was a time of catching up. We all wanted to know how everyone else was doing. Of course, the entire medical team wanted to hear from us. How had the last year been for us? How and what were the children doing? Were there any new happenings? We wanted to hear from them as well, and were so pleased to learn that the hospital continues to grow and thrive. There were new departments, more specialties, and more children being taken care of.

But mostly the occasion was like a family reunion. Debbie served her baked goods. There were laughter and tears – and there was testimony to the grace of God. We engaged in conversation for an hour. Then it was only right that everyone needed to get back to work. After all, we were at Children's, and as always it was filled with hurting and healing kids. The meeting was "adjourned." Slowly, the doctors began to make their way out, but not without more hugs and final words of encouragement and gratitude being exchanged.

Then, to our surprise, Nurse Susan showed up at the door. With the leftover baked goods being distributed to the other nurses on the floor, word had gotten out that the "Landis Parents" were present. Nurse Susan heard this, immediately thought of Darla and her parents, and made a beeline to the conference room. Seeing Susan's smiling face again was such a blessing and brought back so many memories of the excellent care she had given to Darla.

As was only fitting, Mark and Peggy were the last ones to leave. After talking a bit more with them about family life, we brought our visit to a close by holding

hands while Chaplain Mark led in a prayer of blessing. It was all so familiar and so fitting. During a time of stirred up emotions, we were blessed by the gentle and soothing prayer of one who walked with God. Like it had happened so many times before during our 32 days in Birmingham, we once again grasped the truth that was now a part of our thought DNA.

No matter what happens today, God is good.

I will sing the Lord's praise,
for he has been good to me.

Psalm 13:6

Darla Joy Landis
September 17, 1999 – August 24, 2012

David R. Landis has been involved in ministry to Alabama's incarcerated since 1999.
David currently serves as a leader of churches in Southern Alabama. He also enjoys graphic design. David and his wife Deborah have three married children and live in Atmore, Alabama.

Contact: *davidraylandis@gmail.com*

33261925R00084

Made in the USA
Middletown, DE
13 January 2019